No Time to Play:

Youthful Offenders in Adult Correctional Systems

Barry Glick and
William Sturgeon

with Charles R. Venator-Santiago

American Correctional Association Staff

Reginald A. Wilkinson, President

James A. Gondles, Jr. , Executive Director

Gabriella M. Daley, Director, Communications and Publications

Leslie A. Maxam, Assistant Director, Communications and Publications

Alice Fins, Publications Managing Editor

Michael Kelly, Associate Editor

Sherry Wulfekuhle, Editorial Assistant

Production by Morgan Graphics, Takoma Park, Maryland

Printed in the United States of America by Graphic Communications, Inc.
Upper Marlboro, Maryland

ISBN 1-56991-071-5

This publication may be ordered from:

American Correctional Association
4380 Forbes Boulevard
Lanham, Maryland 20706-4322
1-800-222-5646

For information on publications and videos available from ACA, contact
our worldwide web home page at: http://www.corrections.com/aca.

Library of Congress Cataloging-in-Publication Data:

Glick, Barry.
  No time to play: youthful offenders in adult correctional systems
  / Barry Glick and William Sturgeon, with Charles R. Venator-Santiago.
      p.   cm.
  Includes bibliographical references and index.
  ISBN 1-56991-071-5 (pbk.)
  1. Juvenile delinquents—Rehabilitation—United States. 2. Juvenile
  detention—United States. 3. Juvenile justice, Administration of—
  United States. 4. Corrections—United States.
  I. Sturgeon, William.   II. Venator-Santiago, Charles R.   III. Title.
  HV9104.G58   1988
  364.36—dc21   98-9196
                                                                CIP

Contents

Introduction

Between 1992 and 1995, forty-one states passed laws which made it easier for juveniles to be tried as adults. From 1985 through 1994, the number of juvenile cases waived to adult court increased by 71 percent. And much of the current "get tough on crime" rhetoric has been directed at a new breed of juvenile offenders, deemed by the public and policymakers to be more violent and more indifferent to the consequences of their actions than those of a previous generation.

Whether today's juvenile offender is, in fact, more violent, or whether juvenile offenders have become the target for a society outraged by a rising violent crime rate continues to be debated at the highest levels of our criminal justice systems. What isn't under debate, however, is the growing number of juveniles housed in adult facilities, and the desperate need for programming and guidance in managing this population.

No Time to Play: Youthful Offenders in Adult Correctional Systems provides a comprehensive look at this special needs population and the myriad issues facing those entrusted with their care. The management of juvenile offenders, particularly serious, violent juvenile offenders, requires not only an understanding of adolescent development, but a new approach to classification, security, educational programming, and substance abuse treatment. All of these issues and more are addressed in *No Time to Play*, a companion volume to *Managing Delinquency Programs that Work* that was issued in 1995 and which is still very much relevant for those who work with adolescents in both juvenile and adult facilities.

James A. Gondles, Jr.
Executive Director
American Correctional Association

Dedications

To my mother, Dorothy Landan Glick, who provided me with the attitudes, beliefs, skills and values to inherit my world and be successful in it; and to one of my most favorite people, my nephew Eric Halvor Veium, who has taught me much about the adolescents who must grow up in our world today, and who continues to work very hard to develop those attitudes, beliefs, skills, and values to inherit his world, and be successful in it. — BG

To my mother and father, Madeline and Alexander Sturgeon, whose love, understanding, and guidance during my teenage years kept me on the right track; and to my wife, Rose Ann, and son, Patrick, who have always supported my efforts. — WS

To Professors Roberto Alejandro and John Brigham for their incredible support during my graduate career. — CRVS

Preface

Scope and Function of the Book

We have organized this book to provide the fundamental knowledge for policymakers, administrators, managers, supervisors, and direct line staff to explore and apply to their current and immediate future situations. We have included in the introductory section, a history of the systems that are the foundation of our current predicament. Policymakers have decided that violent youthful offenders should be placed in adult corrections systems to make communities safer, programs more effective, systems more efficient, and most critical, to hold these youthful offenders accountable for their actions. Whether one agrees with this policy direction or opposes it, whether one believes such a position is prudent or detrimental, whether one endorses placing young people under the age of eighteen in adult corrections institutions or rather in specialized juvenile centers, is unimportant and unrelated to the paradigm currently being used to serve this population. As such, we end the first section with some different ideas for viewing one's work with this offender population and by offering a plea that those who work with this population consider a change in their own way of thinking.

This book next provides readers with information directed toward expanding their paradigms and forcing a reevaluation of their current thinking. As such, Section Two provides basic information about adolescent development, from a traditional psychosocial frame, but also based on the authors' experiences and expertise.

Section Three deals with the organization, administration, and management issues that need to be addressed when providing programs and services to the violent youthful offender. Such areas as classification and needs assessment, staff selection, supervision, training and development, gang issues and management, and policies and procedures are investigated from the frame of reference of the youthful violent offender placed in adult corrections systems.

Section Four deals with specific programs and services required for those violent youthful offenders with special needs. This manuscript pays attention to those needing special education, and sex offenders, and substance abusers, and examines suicide prevention. This is a critical section since adult corrections systems engage in paradigms which are antithetical to many of the concepts suggested throughout this section. Paradigms will need to be changed and perceptions broadened if we are to be successful with this population.

We end this monograph with a section that reviews current resources and primary organizations that support juvenile justice and adult corrections systems. The last part of the section is devoted to looking at the future and highlighting those issues the system will need to address if it is to be effective when implementing this new policy direction.

Appendices also are provided to equip the reader with a security checklist and special definitions when dealing with this population.

Acknowledgments

There are many people to whom we are indebted for making this project a reality. First to our families who have supported us with their love, devotion and understanding. They were most tolerant during those long hours when we sat by our computers, sometimes oblivious to our surroundings, to complete our work.

We are also greatly appreciative of our colleagues who have helped us with many of our ideas and concept formation. Special thanks to Nancy Shomaker and Alan Ault of the National Institute of Corrections who were sounding boards for our thoughts and opinions throughout. Also, thanks to Commissioner Michael Moore of the South Carolina Department of Corrections, who with his broad smile yet unyielding standards, insured that our premises about youthful offenders were rooted in reality. We are most fortunate to be influenced by Leonard G. Dunston, president, National Association of Black Social Workers, and G. Rosaline Preudhomme, executive director, Fountain for Youth Services, New York City, whose vision for those youth most at risk and those caught up in the grips of the criminal justice systems, remains positive and optimistic.

We wish to acknowledge and thank Dr. Donald Andrews, professor, Carleton University, Dr. Marilyn Van Dieten, clinical psychologist, Ottawa, Canada, and Dr. Patricia Van Voorhis, professor of criminal justice, University of Cincinnati who took time from their precious schedules to read and critique parts of this manuscript.

We especially are indebted to the hundreds of young people who have passed our way, either as incarcerated offenders, or those, like the one to whom this book is dedicated, Eric Halvor Veium, who have taught us about adolescent development and behavior, and the challenge of growing up in a world where guns are the means to arbitration, drug use is a leisure time activity, and ego-centrism is a value considered acceptable. Yet, these are the very same young people who have provided us with the vision and hope that has led to this book. They are the ones who taught us about the alternative culture, the menace of the world they are about to inherit, the basic skills required to survive and be successful, the resilience they must have to withstand peer pressure, antisocial behavior, and criminal influences. It is easier to stray from the expected path than it is to maintain prosocial values and behavior, I have been told by many of these young people. That is why each of us must be thankful when we witness a young person's success, an adolescent's dream realized, and that but one-half of one percent of the adolescent population are the subject of this monograph.

Finally, to our managing editor for this project, Alice Fins of the American Correctional Association, we are most humbly indebted, for it was she who shared our vision and provided the support, faith, and confidence to see this project to its completion.

1 History and Current Realities

Those of us who nostalgically recall the comedy team of Laurel and Hardy probably remember Hardy's famous lines: "This is a fine mess you've got us into!" After saying this, Hardy would fiddle with his tie right in Laurel's face. Well, this is a fine mess we have gotten ourselves into. A small number (less than one-half of 1 percent) of juveniles are committing violent crimes, such that jurisdictions across North America now place these violent youthful offenders into adult correctional systems for their "just deserts."

To fully understand the magnitude of this public policy, we first will review the history and development of the criminal justice system, both adult and juvenile. We then will explore those issues relevant to the violent youthful offender, as reported by jurisdictions across North America, identifying those trends and themes currently being affected in the adult and juvenile corrections systems. We end the section by suggesting that we change our paradigms on youth violence, if we are going to be successful in curbing this most deleterious social condition.

Background and History of the Criminal Justice System

If we do not learn from history, we are destined (doomed) to repeat it. Society has dealt with criminal behavior in a variety of ways ranging from harsh retribution to rehabilitation programs and services. In all cases, the goals were similar: protection of society, preservation of the social order, and deterrence from further criminal activities for those who contemplated antisocial, criminal behavior. We provide the reader with a comprehensive overview of the history and background of the criminal justice system to demonstrate:

- Juveniles have posed special problems throughout history

- Aggression and violence is not a new social problem

- The juvenile justice system was created and is based on certain assumptions about child and adolescent development (See Section Two)

- The criminal justice system has acquired technological and program competencies based upon research, practice, and experience

1

- Corrections public policy has moved, more recently, toward a more conservative, punishment-oriented position—yet corrections policy has vacillated between rehabilitation or treatment-oriented interventions and punishing harsher with little tolerance for prison programs

The Adult Criminal Justice System

In actuality, we can trace the first social sanctions for crimes against society, both property and personal, back to biblical times. The Old Testament is replete with social laws. Violation of these social laws led to an immediate sanction that ranged from public humiliation to death. The Bible was specific to make the punishment fit the crime, as illustrated by the following:

On Murder:

. . . And if he smite him with an instrument of iron, so that he die, he is a murderer: the murderer shall surely be put to death. Or if he smite him with throwing a stone, wherewith he may die, and he die, he is a murderer: the murderer shall surely be put to death. Or if he smite him with a hand weapon of wood, wherewith he may die, and he die, he is a murderer: the murderer shall surely be put to death. The revenger of blood himself shall slay the murderer: when he meeteth him, he shall slay him.
(Numbers 35:16-19)

On Juvenile Delinquency and Incorrigibility:

If a man have a stubborn and rebellious son, that will not hearken to the voice of his father, or the voice of his mother, and though they chasten him, will not hearken unto them; then shall his father and his mother lay hold on him, and bring him out unto the elders of his city, and unto the gate of his place; and they shall say unto the elders of his city: "This, our son is stubborn and rebellious, he doth not hearken to our voice; he is a glutton and a drunkard." And all the men of his city shall stone him with stones, that he die; so shalt thou put away the evil from the midst of thee; and all Israel shall hear and fear.
(Deuteronomy 21:18-21)

On Social Order and Community:

And he that killeth any man shall surely be put to death. And he that killeth a beast shall make it good: beast for beast. And if a man cause a blemish in his neighbor; as he hath done, so shall it be done to him; Breach for breach, eye for eye, tooth for tooth: as he hath caused a blemish in a man, so shall it be done to him again. And he that killeth a beast, he shall restore it: and he that killeth a man, he shall be put to death. Ye shall have one manner of law, as well for the stranger, as for one of your own country: for I am the Lord your G-d.
(Leviticus 24: 17-22)

In Greco-Roman times, citizens usually were banished from the city-states if they violated laws. Generally, harsh physical punishment was reserved for slaves, since they were considered subhuman and were thought to respond only to abuse, if they violated the law. In these early times, interpersonal violence, even death, was perceived to be a private matter, to be reconciled between the aggrieved parties. This latter situation lasted well into the Middle Ages, where there was little or no law or government control. Rather, disputes were settled by family feuds, duels, and vigilante justice. Sometimes, individuals settled their differences as the early Romans did, by using a system of economic sanctions such as fines or forfeitures of property.

After the eleventh century, criminal law and punishment were directed to maintaining the public order. As such, for crimes, even unintentional murder, offenders were given a fine to pacify the injured party and dissuade others from entering into group battles and bloodshed. During this time, there was some standardization that resulted in some common law penal practices. Carried forward from earlier Roman times, capital and corporal punishment typically was given to the poor, while the wealthy were able to buy their way to freedom or exile. During those early times, public humiliation of the perpetrator by flogging, branding, mutilating, and executing was common practice. During these Dark Ages and Middle Ages, the concept of retribution, sadistically applied, to create a public spectacle was the punishment of choice and used to punish rather than create either a deterrent effect or community safety.

With the rise of larger metropolitan areas by the early 1600s, there was a tremendous market for manual labor. As such, criminals now were made to do hard labor, rather than being publicly tortured and maimed. English law changed dramatically during these times to accommodate the new social order. The Poor Laws required the poor and vagrants to work in public or private enterprise. To better manage these work crews, governments established houses of correction. The famous Bridewell Workhouse was built in 1556, and was so popular, that Parliament ordered that a workhouse be built in every English county.

Almost simultaneously, the American colonies needed manual labor. So, many convicts were shipped across the sea to work in the colonies. In 1617, an Order in Council granted a reprieve and stay of execution to anyone convicted of robbery or other felonies who could be employed overseas. Since colony plantation owners paid for the convicts' transportation and services while they performed labor, the English Government favorably transported convicts to America and Australia. The Old Baily Court of London supplied more than 10,000 convicts to the colonies during a sixty-year period.

By the 1800s, there was less need for manual labor, because of the Industrial Revolution. As a result, there was a drastic reduction in the need for manual laborers, and the use of capital punishment dramatically increased, even for the most minor of offenses. Capital punishment was so excessive, that legal activists during that time argued that physically punishing and hanging should be replaced with periods of confinement and incapacitation. As such, workhouses and jails were used to hold petty convicts, the destitute, and vagabonds. Conditions in these places were so deplorable, that the Sheriff of Bedfordshire, John Howard, wrote the *State of the Prisons* (1877), which lead to Parliamentary legislation to build secure and sanitary prisons.

By 1820, long periods of incarceration in reformatories or penitentiaries replaced physical punishment both in England and the United States. While these institutions were considered "liberal social reforms," they quickly became filthy disease-ridden holding facilities. The earlier prisons required inmates to pay for their food and upkeep. Those who could not pay were fed garbage and scraps until they were able to pay for their upkeep or starved to death. Since earlier jails were administered by appointed sheriffs who profited from the difference between what was allocated to their jail and what was actually spent, these individuals provided few services and minimal sustenance.

The first American jail was built in James City, Virginia, in the early 1600s. However, it was William Penn, the Governor of the Pennsylvania Colony who revolutionized the corrections system by banning flogging, mutilating, and physically punishing or torturing inmates. Rather, Penn required felons to be imprisoned at hard labor, with moderate corporal punishment, fines, and forfeiture of property. Each county in the colony was instructed to build a corrections house and was responsible to raise funds to build the jail and provide for operating expenses. Unfortunately, the system reverted back to more brutal ways after Penn died in 1718. Other early penal institutions included the Newgate Prison of Connecticut, and Castle Island Prison built in 1785 in Massachusetts.

Not until after the Revolutionary War did Pennsylvania again endorse the concepts of William Penn. Dr. Benjamin Rush, formed the Philadelphia Society for Alleviating the Miseries of Public Prisons in 1787. Dr. Rush, supported by the Quakers, sought to obtain a level of humane and orderly treatment of those incarcerated in prisons. They argued against the use of the death penalty except for crimes that involved treason, murder, rape, arson, and other heinous acts against society. The Quakers, under the leadership of Dr. Rush, were so successful, that they enjoined the legislature in 1790 to renovate the entire penal system. As a result, facilities at the Walnut Street Jail housed convicted felons and separate cells were built for other more violent felons.

By 1816, New York State built a facility at Auburn. The Auburn Prison was an innovation because it introduced a tier system. Cells were built vertically on five floors of concrete. It also was referred to as *the congregate system*, since prisoners ate and worked in groups. Unruly prisoners were housed separately in a different section of the institution. The

Auburn Prison introduced a philosophy based on fear and punishment, with the ultimate threat of isolation, for those who were most out of control. The concept of solitary confinement was most egregious, since prisoners were isolated, usually in dark dungeon-like conditions, for long periods of time.

Yet another innovation was introduced in 1818 by Pennsylvania, which established a prison that housed prisoners in single cells. There was no need for classification of prisoners since each cell isolated inmates from one another for the duration of their sentence. The Western Pennsylvania Penitentiary was built in a semicircle with the cells positioned along the circumference. Inmates were kept in solitary confinement almost constantly, being allowed to exercise in groups for about one hour per day. A second similarly designed institution, Eastern Pennsylvania Penitentiary was built by 1820, in Philadelphia. These structures were deemed cost-efficient since they reduced the number of prison guards required, isolated inmates, reduced both the services required for prisoners, and the need for group supervision.

Great debates raged during these early times over the merits of the Auburn System versus the Pennsylvania System. Proponents of the Auburn System labeled the Pennsylvania System as cruel and unusual punishment, and inhumane; they suggested that the solitary confinement aspects of this system damaged inmates physically and emotionally. The Auburn System was criticized for allowing inmates to mingle and socialize with one another, often establishing antisocial groups. Ultimately, the Auburn System prevailed and was replicated throughout the United States. Many of its attributes still are used today.

Throughout the nineteenth century, the corrections system in the United States struggled with the best way to manage prisoners, while at the same time administering a cost-effective enterprise that would not burden the law-abiding citizen. Conditions inside the prison deteriorated, and corporal punishment now was conducted indoors, out of public sight.

The congregate care system that was developed at Auburn is remarkably similar to modern systems. However, most prisons at that time were organized around industry and self-sufficiency. Prisons either sold the labor of its inmates to private businesses, who then were supervised by the contractor (known as the *contract system*); or the prison leased its prisoners to a business for a fixed annual fee. This latter system, known as the *convict-lease system*, literally transferred the supervision and control of the inmate from the state to private enterprise. This cheap labor was a windfall for the private entrepreneur, and this practice was sustained until the advent of the trade unions around the 1880s, which were successful in lobbying for legislation to restrict prison labor through interstate commerce regulations and the establishment of laws on use of prisoner services.

At the National Congress of Penitentiary and Reformatory Discipline held in Cincinnati in 1870, Warden Zebulon R. Brockway of the Elmira Reformatory in New York State, advocated for indeterminate sentences, parole, and rehabilitation services for prisoners. He described to the Congress participants a program of services that included remedial education for illiterate inmates, vocational training shops to teach prisoners a skill which they could use when released, a library for reading and research, as well as lectures by professors from local area colleges. The Elmira system appeared very similar to our modern "innovative" boot camp model, in that military-type training was used to discipline prisoners, and there were overarching military principles, which pervaded the inmates' education, manual training, recreation, supervision, movement, and even release decisions.

The Elmira model was extremely popular and attempts were made to replicate it across the country, although systems found it difficult to abandon the prison-industry paradigm. However, in the early 1900s, prisons were deplorable, often crowded, understaffed, and underbudgeted.

Yet, conservatives and state administrators believed that only stern discipline was required to control the prison population. Harsh corporal punishment, used in earlier times including beating and mutilating the body, were abandoned, and gave way to more use of solitary confinement in bare, stark, dark, and dank cells. Reform advocacy groups, such as the Mutual Welfare League, which was begun by Thomas Mott Osborne, argued that prisoners needed to be treated humanely, not isolated from society since they one day would return to it, and needed to be taught skills, which they could use upon release.

This group and others led the way to prison reform. Prisoners were allowed to congregate in the yard and mingle or exercise a few hours each day. Recreation time with movies and radios was permitted, and liberal visiting hours for family and friends were instituted.

With the onset of the Great Depression and World War II, there were greater restrictions on prison industry and manufactured goods. The Sumners-Ashurst Act (1940) made it a federal offense to transport by interstate commerce those goods made in prison that were for private use.

The prison system that evolved by the end the twentieth century is an amalgam of historical development, socioeconomic conditions, and prison administrator innovation. However. besides these, several forces, which converged during a twenty-year period between 1960 and 1980, had an impact on the modern corrections system. After years of laissez-faire policy, state and federal courts began to hear and rule on prisoners' rights issues. In case after case, the judiciary began to mold policy. The courts held that institutionalized prisoners had rights to medical services, procedural due process, basic clean living conditions, and freedom of religion and speech. These actions led to an aggressive and active prisoners' rights movement that recently has been curtailed by more conservative political thinking.

The riots and prison takeovers at Attica (in New York) and at New Mexico State Penitentiary raised public concern about the safety and welfare of the population within the prison and the community in which it was located. Public attention became riveted on behaviors "on the inside." This attention allowed the public to see the potential for death and destruction to staff and inmate alike through the revelations of graphic details of prison murders, rapes, and beatings. The bipolar reaction to this situation either has been to provide greater opportunity for inmate input into prison administration or to build newer maxi-secure prisons to deal with this more violent offender.

Another influence on the operation of the modern penal system was the onset of the meta-analyses of those programs that work and have an impact on prisoner behavior and recidivism. The proclamation by Martinson (1974) that there are no programs that meaningfully impact on recidivism and prisoner criminal behavior—that is, nothing works!—devastated the rehabilitation movement. The conservative position for greater incapacitation and longer periods of incarceration prevailed, such that since the 1980s the prison system has grown in geometric proportions. In New York State, for example, the prison cells for incarceration increased from approximately 25,000 in 1975 to more than 80,000 in 1997. Texas, California, Utah, Nebraska, and Kansas all have had similar proportional increases. Attempts to provide alternatives to incarceration have received little support, and in some cases, have proven detrimental for policymakers. (To wit, the presidential election of 1988 in which George Bush defeated Michael Dukakis, based, in part, on Dukakis' furlough program while Governor of Massachusetts.)

The Juvenile Justice System

For the most part, the juvenile justice system in North America is organized at the state or provincial levels of government. Most juvenile justice systems are structured so that a governmental agency sets standards through established policies and procedures. The functions of budget planning, fiscal control, personnel, establishing program initiatives, and monitoring the quality of care are usually centralized within the agency, whether it be in an office whose chief administrative officer is a supervisor, a division whose head is a director, or in a department whose executive is a commissioner. Each is responsible to the public to provide communities that are safe and a system of programs and services for youth placed in their custody.

The juvenile justice system evolved from the child care institutions of the late nineteenth and early twentieth centuries. As early as 1825, there was a growing concern about the undisciplined behaviors of boys, especially those who were neglected by their families. In 1877, the Charity Organization Society, the Associations for Improving the Condition of the Poor, and other church-affiliated groups began to support larger refuge houses and institutions to care for those children who were without family support or in trouble in their communities. Also, the Society for the Prevention of Pauperism established a house of refuge for these types of youth, an intervention approach subsequently replicated in several urban areas. There was no formal system of rehabilitation or control for delinquents; no one was empowered to send children to these or other institutions, that is until the first juvenile court was established in 1899 in Chicago.

Once juvenile courts were established to protect the health and welfare of children, voluntary child care agencies grew throughout the United States to deal with the delinquents incapable of living at home. By 1925, the training school, a large institution that was self-sufficient and housed delinquent youth from ages seven through twenty-one, was prominent throughout the Northeastern and Southern United States. These institutions often developed into repositories for youth. They relied on rigid regimentation and corporal punishment to control acting-out behaviors, all in the name of rehabilitation and child welfare.

By 1940, many youth advocacy groups, including the American Law Institute, became so concerned with the failures of institutional place-ments for juveniles, that they recommended the establishment of Youth Correction Authorities throughout the United States. The States of California, Massachusetts, Minnesota, Texas, and Wisconsin were the first to heed the recommendation and to form some sort of youth au-thority. The purpose of these youth authorities was to establish a board responsible for considering the special needs of youth and ordering the commitment of youth, for whom it appeared necessary, to the most appropriate institutions that were available. By 1945, states such as New York had formalized their youth commissions into state agencies responsible for youth services and programs.

Thus, the juvenile justice system evolved from a rather informal structure motivated by church people to provide services to the unwanted and the destitute to a multibillion-dollar industry that employs thousands of people to provide services to juvenile delinquents, some of whom have committed the most heinous of crimes. The juvenile justice system of the 1980s relied upon the public and private sectors to provide services to youth. These programs represented an array of community and noncommunity-based residential facilities that were available to local family courts as they disposed of juvenile cases. The administrators of these programs and services were charged with rehabilitating youth placed in their care and returning these youth to communities as productive, effective, and contributing citizens.

By the end of the 1980s and into the early 1990s, youth violence was so uncontrolled in our communities and neighborhoods, even beyond the urban centers into suburbia and rural towns, that policymakers turned toward legislation to resolve the social assault on community and citizen safety. As will be discussed later in this section, legislators passed laws that were harsh on adolescents. These laws punished youth for the crimes they committed without taking into account their age or developmental levels of growth. Adolescents were treated as adults, and not too long after, young offenders no longer were placed in juvenile institutions, but were sentenced as adults to adult prisons and corrections systems. Indeed, in some jurisdictions, such as New York, the juvenile justice agencies established earlier in the century either have been dismantled or incorporated into adult corrections agencies or newly created mega-agencies.

Legal Issues

The justice systems continue to struggle with the public policy position on the treatment of young people who commit heinous crimes in their communities, create unsafe neighborhoods and frighten citizens. By and large, the public is tired of being intimidated, harassed, and physically harmed. The public is impatient with young people who continue to damage property, vandalize neighborhoods, and disregard economic costs to individuals. The public is intolerant of treating violence with nurturing programs for delinquents; and the public now is lobbying legislators to get tough on crime, especially that committed by young offenders. As such, jurisdictions across North America have begun to adjudicate young criminals as adults. This category of youthful offender includes those under the usual age of majority (sixteen to eighteen). Some of these new offenders are as young as ten. These legislative actions are further compounded as jurisdictions also move toward expanding the band of criminal activities for which young people may be sentenced and placed as adults. Indeed, some jurisdictions seriously are considering a complete revision of their juvenile codes and juvenile court systems.

We will explore some of the legislative and statutory positions, which various states, territories, and Canadian provinces have developed in reaction to managing the increasing numbers of violent youthful offenders. This section is concerned with some of the public policy trends for managing violent young offenders. It is our contention that, in general, legislators and lawmakers are struggling to find ways to contain the increasing violence committed by younger offenders. They often are torn between meeting the demands of their constituents, insuring their communities are safe, and preventing the adult justice system from becoming responsible for raising children in prison.

Yet, there is also a position which warns against incarcerating young offenders in adult systems. American Correctional Association Executive Director James A. Gondles, Jr. (1997), in an editorial, summarizes very well the position of those who advocate that kids are kids, not adults.

He states in part:

> Kids are kids, not adults. . . . But it troubles me deeply that our
> focus is on juvenile justice and not juvenile education. It's about
> trials and not about schools or discipline. It's about punishment
> and not about mentoring. It's about dropping mandates and not
> about day care. No, I can't understand it and I don't agree with it.
> We will never, in my view, solve our problems on the back end
> with punishments. We will solve our problems only if we are
> united with a higher purpose of doing better on the front end with
> day care, preschool, schools, churches, other institutions and yes,
> families. Kids are our future and we need to invest in them. Treat-
> ing kids as adults solves very little; it's another quick-fix solution
> to a complex problem that took years to reach and will take years
> to resolve.

To illustrate this dilemma, we will explore issues such as the relationship between age and criminalization; classification categories and legislation on housing of juveniles; adult adjudication of juveniles; and legal
attitudes toward rehabilitation, education, and alternative discipline.
To be sure, the intent is to discern some of the patterns and possible
directions in which lawmakers are directing public policy. In addition,
we will offer some further possible critiques which may enlighten the
reader about some of the possible dangers implicit in these approaches,
especially in light of Mr. Gondles' admonition.

Age and Criminalization

One of the major trends across North America is the decrease in age
for which a juvenile can be prosecuted as an adult and incarcerated in
adult facilities. Also, almost simultaneously, there has been a significant
increase in the number of crimes for which juveniles now are tried as
adults. Moreover, a number of states have incorporated sentencing
guidelines, which provide automatic determinate sentences. The result
increasingly is that younger juveniles are prosecuted as adults, and are
serving longer sentences for certain felonies, often entirely, no matter
how young they are, in adult facilities.

In response to public opinion to hold younger people accountable for
their criminal actions, a significant number of states have lowered their
age for adult adjudication. For example, as an American Correctional
Association survey respondent from Colorado explained:

> The Colorado "Children's Code" is now in the process of a com-
> plete rewrite by the legislature. There would be significant
> changes if the legislation passes in its current form, including a
> significant lowering of the age at which juveniles could be filed
> upon directly in District Court for remanding to the adult system
> (Larry H. Johnson, ACA Survey, February 2, 1996).

Other states also have lowered the age for which a juvenile can be adjudicated as an adult to under the age of fourteen, and include: Florida, Georgia, Iowa, Maryland, Mississippi, Nebraska, New York, North Carolina, Oregon, Washington, and Wisconsin. In Florida, for example:

> A child of any age who is charged with a violation of state law punishable by death or by imprisonment is subject to the jurisdiction of the court as set forth in s. 39049(7) unless and until an indictment on the charge is returned by the grand jury. When such indictment is returned, the petition for delinquency, if any, must be dismissed and the child must be tried and handled in every respect as an adult (Florida Statutes of 1993, § 39.0587 (d)1).

By contrast, in Maryland, there is no presumption of incapacity for a seven-year-old. Thus, in a delinquency proceeding, there is no presumption of incapacity as a result of infancy for a child who is at least seven years old (Annotated Code of Maryland, § 3-805). The national trend is best summarized by a response from Oregon: there is a "get tough on crime" attitude that is sweeping the country (Dan Duren, ACA Survey, February 29, 1996).

As for the expansion of criminal offenses for which a juvenile can be adjudicated as an adult, the Wisconsin legislature has drafted a bill which holds juveniles liable for any criminal activity that violates any state criminal law (1995 Assembly Bill 130, §938.18(3)). In Ohio, House Bill 1 provides mandatory minimum sentences for juveniles who commit certain violent acts. In addition, it imposes an automatic thirty-year mandatory minimum sentence if a youth used, brandished, or clearly indicated possession of a firearm during the commission of a felony-level offense (Executive Summary, H.B. 1).

Although Canada operates under a different juridical system, where the federal Criminal Code of Canada governs criminal cases, and the Young Offenders Act governs provincial matters, there also have been some discussions around the lowering of the age for adult adjudication of young offenders (Anne H. Kimmitt, British Columbia, ACA Survey, January 6, 1997).

Classification Categories and Housing Legislation

The Juvenile Justice and Delinquency Prevention Act (JJDP)(18 U.S.C. 5031- 5042), which governs federal legislation for juveniles in the United States, limits the confinement of juveniles and states that "any inmate who has not attained his/her 18th birthday shall be placed in a non-Federal juvenile facility." Note, however, that in 1998, Congress is debating a juvenile bill that would place violent youthful offenders as young as thirteen into adult federal penitentiaries. Moreover, Title 18 U.S.C. 5039 states that:

> No juvenile committed to the custody of the Attorney General may be placed or retained in an adult jail or correctional institution in which he has regular contact with adults incarcerated because they have been convicted of a crime or are awaiting trial on criminal charges.

A similar policy, which Canada has modified as the Young Offenders Act (YOA), simply establishes that juveniles should be housed in separate units where juveniles are not influenced by adults, neither by sight nor by sound. Arguably, the federal legislation was designed to both protect juvenile inmates from the abuses of adult inmates, and to prevent juveniles from learning new criminal skills in prison. Failure to comply with this legislation, as well as other provisions of the Juvenile Justice and Delinquency Prevention Act, could lead to loss of Federal grants and funding. The problem, which is becoming a trend in the United States, is that those states which have adequate resources to compensate for the loss or reduction of federal funding, may not necessarily comply with the legislation. In fact, a number of states simply lock juveniles in adult facilities without separating the juveniles from adult inmates.

While many states such as California, Connecticut, Delaware Massachusetts, and Illinois have separate juvenile facilities, some states like Michigan are moving to build separate privately operated facilities or "punk prisons" (J. Otis Davis, ACA Survey, March 13, 1996). In fact, Massachusetts has a unique maximum-security facility in Plymouth, which houses juveniles in a separate facility within an adult facility. However, most juvenile facilities have functioned more as detention centers and minimum-to-medium-security facilities.

Yet, with the onslaught of increasingly more aggressive violent youthful offenders, ones who have committed more heinous crimes, institutions need to reassess their physical plant, security, standards, staff training, and procedures. In many jurisdictions, the juvenile system often is perceived to be inadequate to deal with the violent youthful offender. As such, public opinion, policy, and statute, has become more prone to punish and incarcerate; and less tolerant of habilitation and program interventions for these young offenders. An example of this trend can be noted in the following statement:

> Historically, pursuant to Iowa Code Section 904.503, we have transferred a select number of juvenile remands to the state training school until they reached the age of 18. However, we are able to accomplish less and less of these transfers because the state training school is a minimum-custody facility, and the juveniles being remanded are for the most part violent offenders who do not qualify for minimum custody based on application of our standard custody criteria (Jim Felker, ACA Survey, March 20, 1996).

Even when public policy and statute support treatment interventions for youthful offenders, the adult systems' existing procedures many times inhibit appropriate programming. For example, one state's response to the housing needs for their violent youthful offender population stipulates:

> First, after initial reception and orientation process, offenders are classified according to their unique offender characteristics,

and then placed within the institution. The current classification system provides a means for placing offenders in housing areas that pose the least risk to the offender and where the offender would pose the least risk to those already living there. By forcing all serious youthful offenders into one housing area, the classification system would be unable to account for those serious youthful offenders who would be bad candidates for colocation. For example, we believe that many of these serious youthful offenders will have opposing gang affiliations. Under those conditions, housing opposing gang members could pose great risk to both offenders and staff.

Second, many of these offenders will need a variety of programming requirements. The institution runs much more smoothly when treatment and programming needs are also considered when housing decisions are made. Often, offenders who require a certain combination of treatment and programming need to be housed in a location conducive to easy access to the treatment and programming areas. If all serious youthful offenders were housed in one facility, they might not be able to access programming located in another area (Utah Department of Corrections, Housing Strategies for Serious Youthful Offenders, December 1994).

This strategy is further clarified by a classification system that enables:

the classification staff (to) place offenders in housing areas and among other offenders where the risk of injury to both offenders and staff is at a minimum. For example, offenders who have been identified as predatory are not placed with offenders who have been identified as "victim-type" offenders (Utah Department of Corrections, Housing Strategies for Serious Youthful Offenders, December 1994).

Puerto Rico, perhaps because of its territorial relationship to the United States, is exempt from the particular housing requirements of the Juvenile Justice and Delinquency Prevention Act.

The respondents from Canada suggested that housing young offenders has not been a major problem simply because the population of serious young offenders has been significantly low. The Young Offenders Act, however, does provide for temporary housing of juveniles in adult facilities as long as they are separate and apart, and only in extreme situations (Young Offenders Act, § 16.1, 1985).

Adult Adjudication of Juveniles

There is a strong trend across the United States to move away from the transfer hearing process and toward an automatic and/or discretionary adjudication process. This position appears to be closely aligned to the often popular cliche: three strikes and you're out! An example of this attitude is noted in Connecticut's "Serious Juvenile Repeat Offender" legislation (Francis J. Carino, ACA Survey, March 5, 1996). In some ways, juridical policies like this further contributed to the increase of juveniles being remanded to adult dockets throughout the nation. Rosado (1996) also suggests it is fraught with a number of constitutional issues, such as due process and due care, double jeopardy, and cruel and unusual punishment issues.

Nebraska provided the following example of the problems associated with discretionary indictments of juveniles (Nebraska Juvenile Code § 43-247):

> Policies relating to how charges are filed vary from county to county depending on the philosophy and views of the prosecuting attorney. They are essentially the "gatekeeper" in the Nebraska system. It does create problems for the state with regard to JJDPA compliance when juveniles charged with misdemeanor offenses are sentenced as adults (Mark D. Martin, ACA Survey February 27, 1996).

In absence of consistent public policy relative to indicting and sentencing juveniles, there is greater probability for some to raise issues of fairness, equity, and justice. Certainly, Mann (1993) had identified again what FBI Crime Statistics indicate, that the overwhelming majority of juveniles adjudicated as adults are people of color (in others words, African-Americans and Latinos).

Another issue which appears to be of significant importance is what constitutes confessions and what may be considered coercion. It appears that current case law, legislation, and statutory trends, often treat juveniles like adults, but they do not give juveniles all the rights of adults, particularly during the transfer process. In a way, the court assumes the role of in loco parentis, and in many ways establishes a double standard for juveniles who are adjudicated as adults. An interesting example of this attitude can be seen in a fairly recent case in Michigan where the courts established that:

> Failure to take a fifteen-year-old defendant before juvenile division of probate court immediately after his arrest did not render the confession given by the defendant during the two hour delay inadmissible where defendant was charged as [an] adult under automatic waiver rules, defendant confessed in presence of his mother, sister, and brother, defendant was informed of his *Miranda* rights, and no one asked for attorney or requested an end to questioning at any time; statute requiring that juvenile defendants be immediately taken to probate court does not apply in automatic waiver cases. *People v. Spearman* (1992) 491 N.W.2d 606, 195 Mich. App. 434, appeal denied 495 N.W.2d 382, 441 Mich. 885, appeal denied 497 N.W.2d 188, 441 Mich. 929, reversed in part 504 N.W.2d 185, 443 Mich. 870 (Compiled Laws Annotated, § 600.606).

Leo (1996) raises serious concerns in this regard. Specifically: Are juveniles prepared to make informed decisions concerning their *Miranda* rights? Are they more susceptible to police manipulation and coercion?

Rehabilitation, Education, and Alternative Discipline

It appears that there is a general trend to adjudicate juveniles as adults when the criminal justice system decides that rehabilitation is no longer an option. Once it is established that the juvenile cannot be rehabilitated, the logical option is presumed to be adult adjudication and eventual remand to an adult correctional facility. Education often becomes a remedial effort to rehabilitate juveniles once they have been incarcerated within the adult system. However, this is only limited to high school or General Equivalency Degree requirements. Any other forms of higher education have become political battles. Although there has been an interesting movement to employ community forms of alternative discipline (namely through citizens' participation in special probation programs), this movement seems to be in decline.

Yet, a significant number of states have enacted legislation to deal with educational issues affecting juveniles. In California, for example:

> legislation is pending which may require the Department (of Corrections) to raise the reading level for non-high school graduates. Senate Bill 949 refers to an Individual Development Education Act for those 22 years and below; however it has not begun. There is Assembly Bill 1008 addressing any minor 16 or older who is a violent offender to be housed separately until age 18. This bill may directly impact our ability to provide education (John Berecochea, ACA Survey, March 25, 1996).

Other states that have followed similar policy direction include North and South Carolina, New York, Pennsylvania, Wisconsin, Oklahoma, Wyoming, and Puerto Rico. The latter stands out in an interesting way, for in Puerto Rico, education is compulsory through high school. More importantly, juveniles are mandated to participate in educational programs even if they have been adjudicated as an adult (Bureau of Prisons, 1995).

Until recently, the adult corrections system treated youthful offenders similar to the adult general population. That is, whatever educational opportunities were available within the institution, they were afforded to the youthful offender. However, some concerned individuals asked whether these younger offenders were entitled to have the same educational opportunities as mandated by the education laws and regulations of their local jurisdiction. Were youthful offenders, in need of special education and certified as such, mandated to receive those services as stipulated under the Individuals With Disabilities Education Act (IDEA)? Many adult corrections systems ignored those who called for comparable education services in lieu of vocational training programs and general education.

Congress has ended the debate over whether jurisdictions need to provide special education services to the youthful offender population. During the Summer of 1997, Congress reauthorized IDEA for five years. The law guarantees all disabled Americans through the age of twenty-one "a free and appropriate public education." It also insures that appropriate-related special education services be designed and provided to meet the special needs of the individual. The new reauthorization bill explicitly states that the act applies to prison inmates who are otherwise eligible. While prison authorities will not be mandated to screen inmates for learning disabilities, they will be required to provide special education services for those youthful offenders who previously have been identified as disabled and certified as special education students.

Conclusion

As youthful offenders become more prevalent within the adult corrections systems, a range of legal issues will need to be addressed. We suggest some of the more critical areas that should be studied and understood in order for public policy to be determined and implemented. The corrections professional must be aware of the law, but more importantly must understand that public sentiment demands that citizens and communities be safe from random acts of violence and unsafe living conditions caused by young people. Simultaneously, within the institution, staff must insure that young offenders are provided with appropriate housing, programs, safe environments, and nurturing living conditions, all within the procedures of the agency and statutory limitations of the local jurisdiction. This will be a formidable challenge, since youthful offenders (and their advocates) will continue to test the existing systems, based on the youth's developmental needs.

Research, Problems, and Issues Within the Justice System

There are many ways to explore an issue and research a topic. Indeed, a great deal of effort has been devoted to the study of the violent youthful offender in a variety of areas. Criminality and criminogenic factors have been well documented by Andrews, Bonta, and Hogue (1990, 1994). Program design and effective program principles have been discussed by Gendreau (1981), Gendreau and Ross (1981), and Gendreau and Andrews (1994). Meta-analyses of effective programs have been conducted by Andrews (1980), Gendreau and Little (1994), and O'Leary (1977). Incidents of juvenile crimes are reported annually in the FBI Crime Statistics reports. Several organizations have done research and developed position papers on the violent youthful offender populations. These include the American Correctional Association (1997), the Office of Juvenile Justice and Delinquency Prevention (1996), and the American Psychological Association (1994), among others.

We choose to pursue yet a different approach. Rather than repeating the quantitative studies that are so popular in academic and research settings, we have used a qualitative research domain. While some research scientists may not endorse nor approve of our direction, we believe that qualitative research methods, such as surveys and interviews, provide our profession with yet another set of data to be studied, analyzed, and pondered.

Adult Adjudication of Juveniles in the United States and Canada

On February 16, 1996, the American Correctional Association sent a letter requesting information on key issues and concerns relating to juveniles who are remanded to adult jurisdictions and facilities. Some results from that survey were cited in the prior section. The request asked jurisdictions to provide the following:

- State statutes that authorize juvenile remands and the policies that have been developed to carry these out
- An estimate of the number of juveniles in adult facilities, which includes: demographics on gender and race
- Identification of the type of offense that got those juveniles committed to adult systems
- Description of any current or anticipated programs specifically developed for juveniles in adult correctional facilities

The letter requesting this information was sent to the fifty states, the United States Territories, and to the Canadian provinces. Forty states, one territory, and eight Canadian provinces responded by sending a variety of information relating to the issues in question. What follows is a wealth of fascinating policies and trend indicators that are significant to the violent youthful offender issue throughout North America. We have expanded the original scope of the American Correctional Association project and identified eleven different areas which should enable the reader to explore in greater depth and breadth, some of the ways in which justice systems throughout North America are responding to the ever-growing challenges of juvenile violence.

This part of Section One begins with a description of the methodology used to analyze the information received from the American Correctional Association survey. Data are presented in eleven tables, each of which is described and analyzed. All data is presented as percentages and is provided as a ratio within the United States and then in Canada. Trends and system implications also are identified.

Methodology

One of the major problems which researchers in this field face is the lack of readily available information in a standard format. Primarily, this is due to the variety of ways that states respond to criminal violence. It is

17

compounded by the continuous movement of offenders through the judicial system. Additionally, a significant number of respondents clearly stated that juveniles remanded to adult facilities was a fairly new phenomenon and, as such, most states are currently in the process of redefining how they deal with serious juvenile offenders.

Each jurisdiction provided answers to eleven basic questions based on its own system's experience and available data. These areas of inquiry included:

- Has there been an increase of juvenile transfers to adult jurisdictions within the last decade?

- Questions two, three, and four concerned age categories and attempts to identify those strategies employed by the jurisdictions to deal with the various age categories.

- Questions five and six asked respondents to identify the offense categories under which juveniles either were transferred to adult systems or remanded to adult correctional facilities directly from court.

- Questions seven and eight requested information about gender and race/ethnicity of those juveniles transferred to adult systems.

- Question nine concerned housing juveniles remanded to adult correctional institutions.

- Questions ten and eleven asked respondents to identify the problems and issues that resulted from remanding juveniles to adult systems and to identify the programs provided to this group in these institutions.

Data

In the interest of reader convenience, we have put all the tables that relate to the American Correctional Association survey at the end of Section One. Table 1.1 on page 30 reflects a general understanding that the adjudication of juveniles as adults has been increasing within the United States for the past decade. Twenty-eight states documented their information and twenty-five of them suggested that there had been an increase in juvenile transfers, as well as remands, to adult jurisdictions. This was reflected in the consistent development of new legislation, and in many states, the building of new, separate, public and private facilities to incarcerate juvenile offenders. This means that overall, based on those who suggested that there was a difference in juvenile remands, the vast majority of the respondents indicated that there has been an increase in the number of juveniles remanded to adult systems during the past decade. Likewise, according to cover letters and statements, an overwhelming percentage of the United States' respondents suggested that there had been an increase in juvenile transfers or remands to adult institutions.

However, as Table 1.1 shows, only 18 percent of all respondents said that juvenile remands was not a major issue, in contrast with only 10 percent in the United States. The Canadian provinces, for the most part, agreed that in 1996 juvenile remands was not an issue in their system.

In sum, based on the available information, 89 percent of the respondents reported significant increases in juvenile transfers and remands to adult jurisdictions as well as to adult facilities. This suggests three major trends:

- There has been an increase in juveniles committing violent offenses, which require a more severe form of adjudication.

- There clearly has been an increase in the number of juveniles who have been redefined as adults through a formal adjudication process in the United States.

- The traditional juvenile delinquency paradigm has been undermined by an increasing number of juveniles who have committed crimes that traditionally have been associated with adults.

It appears that the separation between juveniles and adults increasingly has been blurred by both an increase in juvenile violence, and a transformation of the criminal justice system in the United States.

Table 1.2a (pages 32-33) shows the major age categories of juveniles that are now in adult systems. Legislation has lowered the ages, as well as expanded the number of offenses for which juveniles can be tried as adults, and in turn, be remanded to adult facilities.

Table 1.2b (pages 34-35) shows the following:

- The standard age categories for juveniles being treated as adults

- Their transfer ages

- The age categories to remand the transferred juvenile/adult into an adult correctional system

It is interesting to note that under Maryland Statutes (Section 3:805), "there is no presumption of incapacity as a result of infancy for a child who is at least seven years old." By contrast, the Connecticut statutes define the age category for adults at age sixteen, while Nevada and Utah suggest that individuals under twenty-one presumably could be adjudicated in juvenile courts. However, the modal age to be considered an adult was eighteen.

The issue of transfer protocols raised a number of important issues. At the "lower" end of the spectrum, Wisconsin stands out as having suggested that a ten-year-old potentially could be transferred to an adult docket, whereas Oregon and Mississippi suggested that juveniles could be adjudicated as adults at age twelve. Five states (10.2 percent overall) have statutes that potentially could transfer a juvenile to an adult jurisdiction.

Florida also indicates that juveniles can be transferred at any time; however, there is not enough information available to fully assess this protocol. The data indicates that overwhelmingly the age has been lowered from eighteen to the fourteen-to-sixteen-year-old age bracket.

Additionally, Florida statute directs each circuit's state attorney to promulgate written guidelines that determine how juveniles should be transferred from juvenile to adult courts. However, the law does not detail the criteria other than the public good requires that adult sanctions be considered. Some of the criteria are illustrated in the eighth and ninth Florida circuit policies: victim impact; if the juvenile has had previous criminal prosecution or currently has pending criminal court cases; patterns of gang involvement; use of firearms; and degree of violence or threatened violence involved in the offense. The Florida Juvenile Justice Advisory Board urges that the decision to transfer should be based on balancing these factors.

The remand category sought to document the ages at which young adults potentially could be remanded to adult facilities. Mississippi indicated that conceivably it could incarcerate the youngest individuals, at age twelve, followed by Washington, Oklahoma, Iowa, and Georgia, which potentially could remand thirteen-year-olds to adult facilities. Most states actually have separate juvenile facilities within their adult correctional systems; however, there seems to be a movement that increasingly remands younger juvenile offenders to adult facilities.

The number of young people who have been remanded to adult facilities suggests several things. First, many states are responding to the increase in juvenile crime and violence by lowering the age of responsibility and remanding younger criminals to adult facilities. (Indeed, the age of majority has been reduced to as young as twelve for some capital crimes such as: New York State Juvenile Offender Law 1978; Georgia SB 400, 401, 1994). Second, perhaps most importantly, it is becoming increasingly more difficult to distinguish the adult from the juvenile, as well as the institutional responses to each of these populations. This seems to be consistent with the national rhetoric advocating a "get tough on crime" policy. Clearly, the data suggests a paradigm shift in the relationship between the juvenile justice system, the adult criminal justice system,and the offender.

Table 1.3 (pages 36-37) categorizes the protocols and/or procedures used in the adjudication of youthful offenders from juvenile jurisdictions to adult courts. The first three categories (automatic transfers, serious juvenile repeat offenders, and discretionary adjudication) are expressly related, and in a number of states and provinces, the differences are questionable. However, they do represent three different principles. More than 28 percent of the United States respondents, 41 percent overall, indicated that they have a statute that automatically transfers juveniles who have committed specific serious felonies (usually murder and other violent crimes) to their respective adult jurisdictions.

The public policy of automatic transfers appeared to be related, at least in principle, to the notion of the recidivist repeat offender, or serious juvenile repeat offender (SJRO). This category echoes in many ways the "three strikes and you're out" rhetoric that increasingly has become a popular political slogan for "get tough on crime" politicians. For the most part, this means that if juveniles have been convicted of at least two or three prior offenses during the same year as they are being adjudicated for a subsequent offense, they will be considered serious juvenile repeat offenders, and in some states, they automatically will be transferred to an adult jurisdiction. (Connecticut has indicated that there are some constitutional issues that need to be explored.) Interestingly, 34 percent of United States respondents, 29 percent overall, indicated that they have this type of statute.

The third category, which is closely related to the latter, is the discretionary adjudication process. This essentially places the power to transfer a juvenile from a juvenile jurisdiction to an adult court, in the hands of either a judge, or in some cases, a prosecuting attorney. Accordingly, 22 percent in the United States, 29 percent overall, indicated that this process is followed. Two interesting variations indicated that in some states (29 percent), and throughout Canada (100 percent), all juveniles automatically are transferred to an adult court wherein they then undergo a transfer hearing, which could remand them back down to a juvenile jurisdiction. In some instances, 12 percent United States, 10 percent overall, the respondents indicated that there was a concurrent jurisdiction, wherein the prospective merit would be assessed, and the court would make a decision to either prosecute or remand the individual to either court. This policy suggests that the prosecuting attorney conceivably could choose the most appropriate court, as well as accelerate the process. Another issue worth mentioning is that of dual jurisdiction. This model directs that juvenile proceedings commence in juvenile court, and eventually, when juveniles reach the age of majority, they could be tried in an adult court for the remainder of the charges.

Perhaps, the most popular and systematic way used to adjudicate juveniles as adults is a transfer hearing process; 78 percent in the United States, 80 percent overall, indicated that they followed this type of procedure. Typically, it consists of the following:

1. There is a petition by the prosecuting attorney, the offender, or the judge, to transfer the juvenile to an adult jurisdiction.
2. This is followed by a probable cause, an evidentiary, or a prospective merit hearing/disposition.
3. The judge determines whether to proceed with a transfer hearing, and subsequently can remand a juvenile to an adult jurisdiction.

Clearly, there are some variations from state to state; however, this is the basic structure of the protocol. Moreover, it seems that the procedure operates to both increase the efficiency of the court, and to improve the chances that the state will win its case. The second phase is a dispositional hearing wherein the prosecuting attorney seeks to define the prospective merit of the case, whether there is probable cause that the juvenile committed the alleged offense, or simply to establish the available evidence. Again, where the procedure may vary from jurisdiction to jurisdiction, the judge assesses the information and determines whether there is enough cause to have a transfer hearing.

Before the transfer can occur, however, the court usually has the burden to consider some or all of the following:

1. Whether the juvenile is mentally retarded/ill, or should be committed to a mental health institution
2. The nature and seriousness of the offense
3. The extent of the offense and whether it has caused damage to property or people, paying more attention to injuries against persons
4. The treatments, rehabilitation facilities, or alternative institutions available to treat the juvenile, and the rehabilitative potential of the juvenile, as well as his or her prior history of rehabilitation
5. The mental and physical maturity of the juvenile
6. The juvenile's or the community's interests and the public safety in relation to the adjudication
7. Previous records and delinquent activity of the juvenile
8. Whether there was a dangerous weapon or firearm involved
9. The family, home, environment, patterns of living, lifestyle, and the resulting emotional attitude
10. The age of the juvenile and the psychological problem reports
11. The degree of criminal sophistication
12. The nature and circumstances for which transfer is sought
13. Whether the offense was committed in a violent, premeditated, willful or aggressive manner
14. Educational history
15. Available alternative forms of adjudication or ways to deal with the juvenile
16. Whether the juvenile will disrupt, endanger, or pose a threat to other juveniles in a juvenile facility
17. Adequacy of punishment
18. The victim's safety
19. Whether the offense was committed within school premises
20. Other relevant factors

Again, depending on the court or state, the judge may require the prosecuting attorney to demonstrate that the juvenile needs to be adjudicated in an adult court. This is critical, for 51 percent in the United States,

55 percent overall, of the respondents indicated that once a juvenile is transferred, the decision becomes final, and the offender subsequently is adjudicated as an adult in all further proceedings. Only 27 percent in the United States, 35 percent overall, indicated that this decision is appealable.

Among the states and jurisdictions, Delaware stands out in a peculiar way. All transfers and remands are closely scrutinized and evaluated on an individual basis. This resulted in almost no transfers and remands. This raises an interesting question: is there a difference in transfers and remands between states with more available resources and states with fewer resources? Stated differently, will available resources influence the transferring trends by enabling more individualized attention and interventions with juvenile offenders? In a sense, it is almost as if correctional facilities are expected to deal with the problems that no one else has been able to solve without having access to significant resources.

Alternative forms of adjudication are, for the most part, community-based strategies outside of the prison system. Respondents (22 percent U.S.; 31 percent overall) indicated that they potentially could rely on alternative forms of adjudication.

In summary, the data in Table 1.3 indicate that the majority of respondents rely on a transfer-hearing process that seeks to transfer the juvenile to an adult jurisdiction. However, there is an increasing trend to move towards an automatic or discretionary adjudication, particularly in those jurisdictions where the juvenile population is growing and the courts are burdened with cases. This latter movement well may be correlated with some form of serious juvenile repeat offender status. We caution, however, that these transfer protocols need to be scrutinized and subjected to constitutional law, for it appears there is an increasing potential that juveniles may be denied their civil rights throughout the adult adjudicatory process. It seems that, in general, the transfer process in fact may be "overcriminalizing" some juvenile offenders. On the other hand, this option may be viewed by politicans as the only possible way to reduce the level of violence that these offenders now commit.

Table 1.4 (pages 38-39) documents the offenses for which juveniles could be adjudicated as adults. Eighty-five percent of the United States respondents (71 percent overall) reported that those juveniles they transfer to adult dockets have committed crimes, which, if committed by adults, would be considered felonies; and in certain states, punishable by death or life imprisonment (see Appendix 1). What is striking about this information is how little consistency exists across the systems. Some jurisdictions, such as Mississippi, classify traditional juvenile delinquency acts as adult acts, and adjudicate young offenders to adult systems for such acts. Others, such as West Virginia, report they would prosecute and punish young juveniles for capital crimes such as treason (that is, they would seek the death penalty); however, only Texas had a youth under sixteen on death row.

Another alarming statistic is that street gang activity appears to be increasing. While this offense has not been codified in most states, a significant number of states did mention that gang activity was becoming a serious problem that requires more attention. To be sure, a number of respondents suggested that gang activity usually is associated with a number of other offenses increasingly committed by juveniles.

Table 1.5 (pages 40-41) provides data on the number of juveniles in each offense category for which the juveniles could be transferred to adult jurisdictions. The data again support what we know to be generally true:

- More juveniles are being adjudicated for committing acts of violence against people as opposed to committing property crimes.
- Juveniles are being classified within the context of adult categories; in effect, their behavior increasingly appears to be measured by adult standards of violence.

Table 1.5 provides further insight into the nature of violence for which juveniles are adjudicated as adults. Based on the available information, physical crimes against persons comprise the highest category of offenses. The robbery and burglary (R&B) offenses constitute 35 percent and capital and assault and battery (A&B) cases constitute 18 percent individually in the United States, while in Canada robbery and burglary are only 10 percent. This information suggests that juveniles transferred to adult jurisdictions are committing more violent crimes against people than any other offense.

Who actually is being transferred and remanded to adult facilities? The data in Tables 1.6 and 1.7 (pages 42-45) indicate that males comprise 95 percent and females 5 percent of the juveniles remanded to adult correctional systems in the United States. In Canada, males comprise 86 percent and females 14 percent of the young offenders transferred to adult correctional systems. Our data indicates that blacks comprise 58 percent of the juveniles being transferred as adults in the United States adult correctional system. Canada did not indicate that it had a black juvenile population in its adult correctional system. Based on the available information, young black men comprise 56 percent and young black women comprised slightly more than 1 percent of the juvenile population in the adult correctional system in the United States. This minority overrepresentation within the criminal justice system is an issue that concerns many individuals, including civil rights advocacy groups.

By contrast, whites comprised 29 percent in the United States, and 44 percent in Canada, of the juveniles in the adult correctional system. White men and white women comprised 19 percent and 0.4 percent, respectively, of the transferred and remanded populations in the adult United States correctional system. Based on the available information, whites comprised the second largest population in the criminal justice system.

The third largest population represented Hispanics who comprised less than 6 percent of the juvenile population in United States adult correctional care. Canada did not indicate that it had a Hispanic population.

Native or Aboriginal Americans comprised only 0.7 percent of the remanded United States population. However, this group was 34 percent of the Canadian juvenile population remanded to the adult correctional systems.

The least-represented group is the Asian population, which comprise 0.2 percent of the United States correctional population. Canada did not indicate that it had any Asian juveniles in their adult correctional system.

We advise cautious interpretation of the data, which presumes causation and relationships among gender, race/ethnicity, age, and the adjudication process especially since not all jurisdictions reported information in all categories. Despite this, we can discern some trends. The data indicates a disproportionate number of African-American male juveniles are in the adult correctional system; however, this system also contains juveniles who were Caucasians, Hispanics, Native Americans, and Asians. The FBI Crime Statistics Reports and the Bureau of Justice Statistics conjecture about this disproportionate minority representation in the corrections literature.

Table 1.8 (pages 46-47) reports where these young offenders are being housed. The methodological problems in compiling and analyzing these data have been discussed earlier. An additional factor includes those adult correctional facilities with separate juvenile facilities within their walls. Fifty-six percent of United States respondents and 61 percent overall indicated that although they could house young offenders in adult facilities, they try to hold them in juvenile facilities until the age of majority or until they begin to present problems for the facility. Yet, 66 percent in the United States and 69 percent overall indicated that they either house or could house young offenders who have been adjudicated to adult jurisdictions. Although only 7 percent of United States respondents stated that they follow federal law and regulations, (Juvenile Justice and Delinquency Prevention Act), we wonder whether a significant majority of states actually follow or try to follow the stipulated protocol.

Virtually all of the Canadian respondents indicated that they followed the Young Offenders Act (YOA) policies. The Young Offenders Act, as described earlier in the section, establishes that juveniles should be housed in separate units where they are not exposed to adults nor influenced by them, either by sight or sound. The act also establishes that certain violent offenses committed by juveniles require that they be adjudicated and treated as adults. Two respondents (5 percent in the United States, 4 percent overall) explicitly stated that they either were relying on private facilities or in the process of contracting with a private facility to house their juvenile offender population.

Thirty-four percent of the United States respondents and 43 percent overall indicated that they separate their young offender population (who range between the ages of eighteen to twenty-one), and keep this population away from adult contacts. Virtually all of the Canadian respondents indicated that they follow the separate and apart protocol. Nonetheless, a significant number of states suggested that enforcing this policy was problematic because of lack of space, lack of specialized staff, and, in general, because of a lack of adequate resources.

An important issue was raised by some of the respondents regarding the logic of placing young offenders together based on age. Some United States respondents indicated that many of their young offenders belonged to rival gangs and often would present more of a menace to each other if they were housed together rather than being placed in the general population. For example, 32 percent of United States and 27 percent overall indicated that it made more sense to classify young offenders based on such categories as "predator" and "victim." Yet, this, in turn, raises other issues such as whether we can apply these categories to juveniles, for a "predator" on the "outside" easily can become a "victim" on the "inside."

Fifteen percent of the United States respondents and 20 percent overall indicated that they *temporarily* may house juveniles in adult facilities for *brief* periods of time. Clearly, this is precipitated by special circumstances, and virtually all of those who indicated that they had engaged in these practices made it clear that they followed the separate sight and sound protocol, whenever possible.

The data suggests some basic trends. First and foremost, the majority of respondents indicated that potentially they could house young offenders in adult facilities. Second, a significant number of respondents indicated that it made more sense to classify juveniles according to each jurisdiction's classification system. As such, juveniles would be placed according to existing system criteria within the general population, regardless of their age, or physical, or mental maturity. There may be increased activity to house young offenders using the private sector. However, the data is not clear on this issue. Finally, one needs to question the classification protocol in the face of the issues of security among juveniles (in other words, which is the lesser of two evils, adult role models or threatening peers?).

Although 82 percent of the respondents did not offer any explicit information regarding the problems and issues which arise out of the juvenile remands in adult facilities, the responses raise some serious issues as shown in Table 1.9. (pages 48-49). The Canadian respondents did not provide any information.

The two issues most frequently mentioned were gang-related violence and safety concerns for juveniles. Respondents suggested that rival gang violence was a major problem among juvenile offenders. Respondents also suggested that remanded juveniles are simply too young to be in the general population, and it is often quite difficult to guarantee their safety from older prisoners.

Other reported problems and issues include: older inmates raping young offenders; employing the classification protocol designed for adults to these youthful offenders; administering the separate sight and sound federal regulations; designing, developing, and implementing separate program-ming; and complying with the Juvenile Justice and Delinquency Preven-tion Act.

Of particular interest were the issues Washington State raised when incarcerating juveniles in their adult system. These included: the survival of young offenders; the transition of young offenders into the general population; and the lack of educational and social skills among young offenders. Moreover, respondents indicated that young offenders demand more attention from correctional officers and often times they do not behave in the manner in which adults are expected to behave. Puerto Rico indicated that suicide was a major problem. At the very least, the data support our position that it is quite dangerous for young offenders to be housed in adult facilities.

Table 1.10 (pages 50-51) documents some of the programming that occurs in adult facilities (See also Appendix 2). The goal of many of these programs is to rehabilitate individuals, while others appear to be part of the corrections paradigm. Noteworthy is the fact that 37 percent of the United States respondents (41 percent overall) indicated that they offered no special programming for juveniles remanded to adult facilities. For the most part, the other major forms of programming are basic education and vocational education as well as alcohol and drug abuse treatment. Few jurisdictions indicated that they offered counseling for parents, victim awareness counseling, or suicide prevention.

It appears that most respondents do not pay much attention to pro-grams, particularly innovative and targeted programming for young offenders. This may suggest that young offenders who are remanded to adult systems, in fact, may be serving long sentences, if not natural life, which further discourages prison officials from even bothering with rehabilitation.

Conclusion

The issue of juvenile transfers and remands to adult correctional systems and facilities should be of great concern. As a result of the 1995 ACA Survey, the 1996 ACA Survey, and the Office of Juvenile Justice and Delinquency Prevention Testimony (1994), the following trends may be identified:

1. The data indicate an increase in transfers and remands of juveniles to adult jurisdictions and facilities.

2. The age categories, which are being applied to juveniles to transfer them to adult jurisdictions, increasingly are blurring the lines separating the child from the juvenile and from the adult. It is almost as if the juvenile age category (for juvenile delinquents) slowly is being eroded.

3. Younger juveniles increasingly are being remanded to adult facilities.

4. Some adjudication protocols appear to be criminalizing the young offender beyond the scope of their crimes.

5. Imposing adult norms on juveniles eventually will create hybrid inmates with more social, emotional, and interpersonal problems.

6. Offense categories for which a juvenile may be transferred to an adult jurisdiction may be expanding as age categories are lowered.

7. Juveniles commit more violent offenses against persons.

8. Young black men and women disproportionately are transferred to adult jurisdictions and remanded to adult facilities.

9. More young offenders potentially could be locked up in adult facilities than in juvenile facilities.

10. There seems to be a move away from the Juvenile Justice and Delinquency Prevention Act, although it appears that only those states with sufficient resources that can afford to forgo federal funding question this law and ensuing regulations.

11. Young offenders' safety in adult facilities appears to be the major problem challenging officials in adult facilities.

12. There does not seem to be a concerted effort to develop innovative programming for remanded juveniles.

13. The boundaries of the adult, as a "reasoning and responsible" individual, are being consistently redrawn to encompass younger and younger persons.

Changing Paradigms

Many futurists (Barker, 1993; Zeigler, 1973) urge policymakers, strategists, and direct-line workers to expand their horizons and view their world differently. What we think and believe directly impacts on our problem solving and approaches to daily tasks. Try the following:

- Choose a number between one and ten.
- Multiply your choice by nine.
- Separate the digits (for example, if your answer is eighteen, think of it as one and eight).
- Add the digits together.
- Subtract five.
- Convert the answer to its alphanumeric equivalent. (in other words, 1=a; 2=b; 3=c; 4=d, and so on).
- Think of the name of a country that begins with that letter.
- Identify the second letter in that country's name.
- Think of an animal that begins with that letter.
- Now, think of a color for that animal.

Chances are, you identified a gray elephant from Denmark! Between 60 and 90 percent of individuals who complete this exercise will choose a gray elephant from Denmark because of the paradigms we use. Barker (1990) defines paradigms as those rules and limitations we have learned that direct how we think and how we approach problem solving.

Here is another example for you to consider. Read the following sentence and spend no more than thirty seconds looking at it:

The finished files are the result of years of scientific studies combined with the experience of many of the years to come.

How many "F's" did you see? You probably saw less than seven. We all have scotomas, that is blind spots, which prevent us from perceiving what actually is. We have been taught to read with a certain paradigm, a certain set of rules and parameters. The reading paradigm often used is phonetics in which we are taught to pronounce the letter **F** as in **father**. Yet, the **F** in **of** is pronounced as a **V**. We have a scotoma to those **F's** which appear in the word **of**. These rules inhibit us from seeing what is there—that there are seven **F's** in the phrase above.

Barker refers to this as *Paradigm Paralysis*, which causes us to be unable to look at alternatives to our current operations. Our perceptions are influenced strongly by our paradigms, and because we get so good at using our paradigms, we resist changing them. It usually takes someone from the "outside" to help us change these paradigms. This may take the form of training and seminars, private consultants, or administrators external to the organization.

While all people tend to resist changing their paradigms, those who do choose to change from their old paradigms to the new, do so as an act of faith, rather than as a result of available data. There is not sufficient data to convince individuals to change their paradigms during the early stages of new paradigm implementation. Yet, those who do change to a successful new paradigm gain new vision and new strategies to solve problems. With a new paradigm, all involved are on a level playing field so that the practitioners of the old paradigm, who may have had advantage over others, lose much if not all of their leverage and position of power.

Incorporating a new paradigm is just one of the requirements for correctional staff to serve effectively the youthful offenders incarcerated in adult systems. The staff also need to have a comprehensive knowledge of adolescent development and the ability to apply this information to their daily interactions with this population.

TABLE 1.1
Number of Juveniles Held as Adults: 1985-1996*

	No Info.	Increase	Not Problem	1985	1986	1987	1988	1989	1990	1991	1992	1993	1994	1995	1996
UNITED STATES															
Alaska	■														21
Alabama	■												372	505	305
Arizona		■								31	60	65	114	117	
Arkansas		■								152	178	163	214	241	
California	■														395
Colorado		■								14	12	19	40	65	23
Connecticut		■								1,554**	1,458**	1,546**	1,870**	2,073**	2,022**
Delaware			■										2	1	
Florida				307	281	1,181	470	636	797	757	655	719	779	652	4,982**
Georgia	■													105	76
Idaho	■														35
Indiana	■														81
Iowa		■								5	28	30	30	67	23
Kansas												118	101	126	35
Kentucky			■												2
Louisiana		■								46	59	58	72	67	148**
Maryland		■								66	91	85	109	128	
Michigan		■			40	48	80	72		73	107	88	170	154	154
Minnesota		■								28	47	37	53	75	21
Mississippi		■								98	117	132	188	248	147
Missouri		■								18	45	24	24	29	
Nebraska		■								74	73	84	73	117	99
Nevada	■														41
New Mexico		■										7	25	28	49
New York		■		6	25	19	28	21	24	14	10	7	27		195
N. Carolina		■								165	174	172	188	187	3,101**
N. Dakota			■												6
Ohio		■								2	62	17	85	94	119

* All data are a combination of the 1995 and 1996 ACA surveys.
** Data represent juveniles 21 and under.

	No Info.	Increase	Not Problem	1985	1986	1987	1988	1989	1990	1991	1992	1993	1994	1995	1996
Oklahoma		■								43	80	88	75	106	72
Oregon	■													39	20
Pennsylvania		■								34	39	47	62	72	75
S. Dakota			■								7			4	6
Tennessee	■														42
Texas		■					137	149	161	208	279	347	249	502	250
Utah		■													26
Vermont		■								46	49	33	35		
Virginia		■													415
Washington									7	30	41	47	82	95	95
W. Virginia		■												5	
Wisconsin									39	67	80	111	102	139	139
Wyoming	■														20
Total	**10**	**23**	**4**	**313**	**306**	**1,240**	**683**	**886**	**1,108**	**3,546**	**3,759**	**4,057**	**5,157**	**6,052**	**13,245**

U.S. TERRITORIES

	No Info.	Increase	Not Problem	1985	1986	1987	1988	1989	1990	1991	1992	1993	1994	1995	1996
Puerto Rico	■														

CANADA

	No Info.	Increase	Not Problem	1985	1986	1987	1988	1989	1990	1991	1992	1993	1994	1995	1996
B. Columbia			■												5
Manitoba	■														10
New Brunswick			■												19
New Foundland	■														
Nova Scotia			■												
Ontario			■												
Quebec	■														
Yukon			■												
Total	**3**		**5**												**34**

TABLE 1.2a
Number of Juveniles Held as Adults by Age Category in 1996

	No Info.	12	13	14	15	16	17	18	Other	Total
UNITED STATES										
Alaska	■									21
Alabama					5	32	105	163	1,413	1,718*
California						2	39	354		395
Colorado	■									23
Connecticut					1	99	320	433	1,169	2,022*
Florida	■									4,982
Georgia			2	3	28	43				76
Idaho										35
Indiana	■									81
Iowa										23
Kansas						7	28			35
Kentucky	■									2
Louisiana										148
Michigan					36	118				154
Minnesota										21
Mississippi					10	35	102			147
Nebraska					8	14	35	42		99
Nevada										41
New Mexico	■									49
New York	■									195
N. Carolina	■									3,101*
N. Dakota	■									6
Ohio					1	20	98			119
Oklahoma	■									72

* Data represent juveniles 21 and under.

	No Info.	12	13	14	15	16	17	18	Other	Total
Oregon	■									20
Pennsylvania	■									75
S. Dakota	■									6
Tennessee						8	34			42
Texas						5	245			250
Utah	■									26
Virginia					2	77	336			415*
Washington			1	3	4	29	58			95
West Virginia	■									5
Wisconsin						30	109			139
Wyoming	■									20
Total	**16**	**0**	**3**	**6**	**95**	**519**	**1,509**	**1,013**	**2,582**	**14,658**

U. S. TERRITORIES

Puerto Rico	■									

CANADA

	No Info.	12	13	14	15	16	17	18	Other	Total
B. Columbia	■									5
Manitoba	■									10
New Brunswick		1			3	15				19
New Foundland	■									
Nova Scotia										0
Ontario	■									
Quebec	■									
Yukon	■									
Total	**6**	**1**			**3**	**15**				**34**

TABLE 1.2b
Youth Remanded to Adult Facilities by Age

	No Info.	Juvenile	Adult	Transfer	Remand	YOA
UNITED STATES						
Alaska					Before 20	
Alabama				14-25	Before 25	
Arkansas		14	18	14-18		
California			18	16-18	Before 21	
Colorado		18/19	18/19	14-18/19		
Connecticut		-16	16	14-21	14-21	
Delaware		-18	18	-18	-18	
Florida				Any age		
Georgia		-17	17+	13-17	13-17	
Hawaii	■					
Idaho				Any time-18		
Illinois			17+		After 17	
Indiana		-18	18	Under 18		
Iowa			18	13-18	13-18	
Kansas		10 - 18	18	14-18	16+	
Louisiana		-17	17	14-17	Under 20	
Maryland		After 7	18	Under 18	14-21	
Michigan			17	14-17	17+	
Minnesota			18	14-18		
Mississippi			18	12 to 17	12+	
Nebraska		-18	19	P.A. Disc.	19	
Nevada		Less 18 or 21	18	14-18	-18	
New Mexico			18	15-18	-21	
New York		13+	18	16-21	16-21	
N. Carolina				13+	19-21	
N. Dakota				14-16		
Ohio		-18	18	14-21	14-21	
Oklahoma		-17	18	13-18	13-18	

	No Info.	Juvenile	Adult	Transfer	Remand	YOA
Oregon		12 to 25	18	12 to 17	18 -20	
Pennsylvania		12 to 18	18	15 - 17	-18	
S. Carolina		-17	18	16-25	Any time	
S. Dakota				16+		
Tennessee			18	16+	16+	
Texas			18	14-17	16-21	
Utah		Less 18 or 21	18 or 21	14-21	14-21	
Virginia			18	14-18	14-18	
Washington			18	13-18	13-21	
West Virginia		Less 18	18	14-18	18	
Wisconsin		Less 17 or 18	18	10 to 14 or 15+	16 - 21	
Wyoming		12 to 18	18	14-17		

U.S. TERRITORIES

	No Info.	Juvenile	Adult	Transfer	Remand	YOA
Puerto Rico		-21	18	-18		

CANADA

	No Info.	Juvenile	Adult	Transfer	Remand	YOA
B. Columbia		12 to 17	18	14 - 18	-18	■
Manitoba		12 to 17	18	14 - 18	-18	■
New Brunswick		12 to 17	18	14-18	-18	■
New Foundland	■					
Nova Scotia		12 to 17	18	14-18	-18	■
Ontario			18	16/17 - 18	16-20	■
Quebec		12 to 17	18	-18	-18	Amended
Yukon		12 to 17	18	14-18	-18	■

TABLE 1.3
Adjudication Protocols/Procedures for Youthful Offenders

	No Information	Automatic	Serious Juvenile Repeat Offenders	Discretionary	Juvenile Remand	Concurrent Jurisdiction	Dual	Transfer Hearing	Individual Case	Permanent	Appeal	Alternative
UNITED STATES												
Alaska								■				
Alabama								■		■	Yes	
Arkansas			■			■		■		■	Yes	
California	■											
Colorado			■					■		■		■
Connecticut		■	■					■		■	Yes	■
Delaware									■			
Florida		■	■	■				■		■		
Georgia		■			■						Yes	
Hawaii	■											
Idaho				■				■		■	Yes	
Illinois	■											
Indiana		■	■			■		■				
Iowa				■								
Kansas		■	■					■		■		
Louisiana			■					■		■		
Maryland								■		■		
Michigan		■				■		■				
Minnesota		■			■			■		■		
Mississippi					■			■		■		
Nebraska				■	■	■		■			Yes	■
Nevada		■	■	■						■		
New Mexico		■	■									■
New York				■				■				
N. Carolina				■				■		■		
N. Dakota								■		■		
Ohio		■	■					■				
Oklahoma		■			■			■		■	Yes	■

	No Information	Automatic	Serious Juvenile Repeat Offenders	Discretionary	Juvenile Remand	Concurrent Jurisdiction	Dual	Transfer Hearing	Individual Case	Permanent	Appeal	Alternative
Oregon		■						■		■	Yes	■
Pennsylvania					■			■				■
S. Carolina	■									■		
S. Dakota								■		■	No	
Tennessee								■		■		
Texas		■	■		■			■		■	Yes	
Utah					■			■				
Virginia			■		■			■		■	Yes	
Washington			■					■				
West Virginia			■				■	■			Yes	
Wisconsin		■	■		■			■				■
Wyoming					■	■		■				■
Total	4	12	14	9	12	5	1	31	1	21		9

U.S. TERRITORIES

	No Information	Automatic	Serious Juvenile Repeat Offenders	Discretionary	Juvenile Remand	Concurrent Jurisdiction	Dual	Transfer Hearing	Individual Case	Permanent	Appeal	Alternative
Puerto Rico	■							■				

CANADA

	No Information	Automatic	Serious Juvenile Repeat Offenders	Discretionary	Juvenile Remand	Concurrent Jurisdiction	Dual	Transfer Hearing	Individual Case	Permanent	Appeal	Alternative
B. Columbia		■			■		■	■		■	Yes	■
Manitoba		■			■		■	■		■	Yes	■
New Brunswick		■			■		■	■		■	Yes	■
New Foundland	■	■			■							
Nova Scotia		■			■			■		■	Yes	■
Ontario		■			■			■				
Quebec		■			■		■	■		■	Yes	■
Yukon		■			■		■	■		■	Yes	■
Total	1	8			8		5	7		6		6

TABLE 1.4
Offenses for Which Juveniles Are Adjudicated as Adults

	No Info.	Capital	Robbery/Burglary	Sex Crime	Kidnap	Felony	Weapons	Assault & Battery	Drugs	Gangs	Terrorism	Public Offense	Arson	Escape	Vehicular	Schools	Witness	Riot	Shoplifting	Treason	Extortion	Other
UNITED STATES																						
Alaska		■	■	■	■	■																
Alabama		■				■	■		■													
Arkansas		■	■	■	■	■	■		■	■	■	■										
California		■	■	■	■	■	■	■				■	■	■	■							■
Colorado		■				■		■														■
Connecticut		■	■	■		■	■	■	■			■	■									
Delaware	■																					
Florida		■	■	■	■	■	■	■		■			■									
Georgia		■	■	■		■	■	■	■				■									■
Hawaii	■																					
Idaho		■	■	■		■		■					■		■							
Illinois	■																					
Indiana		■	■	■	■	■	■	■	■	■		■	■		■							■
Iowa	■																					
Kansas				■		■	■		■					■								
Louisiana		■	■	■	■	■	■	■	■													■
Maryland		■	■	■	■	■	■	■	■						■							
Michigan		■	■	■		■	■	■	■													
Minnesota		■	■		■	■	■	■														■
Mississippi		■	■	■		■	■	■	■				■						■			
Nebraska		■	■	■		■	■	■	■		■	■	■	■	■							
Nevada		■	■	■		■	■	■	■						■							■
New Mexico		■	■	■	■	■	■	■					■		■							
New York		■	■	■	■	■		■					■									
N. Carolina						■																
N. Dakota		■			■	■	■	■	■				■									
Ohio		■	■	■	■	■	■	■					■									
Oklahoma		■	■	■	■	■	■	■	■				■	■	■							■

	No Info.	Capital	Robbery/Burglary	Sex Crime	Kidnap	Felony	Weapons	Assault & Battery	Drugs	Gangs	Terrorism	Public Offense	Arson	Escape	Vehicular	Schools	Witness	Riot	Shoplifting	Treason	Extortion	Other
Oregon		■	■	■	■	■	■	■					■	■								■
Pennsylvania			■	■	■	■	■	■	■							■						
S. Carolina						■																
S. Dakota			■	■	■		■	■	■				■									
Tennessee		■	■	■	■																	
Texas		■				■		■														
Utah		■	■	■	■	■	■	■	■				■	■	■	■	■	■				■
Virginia		■	■	■	■	■	■	■	■				■	■								■
Washington		■	■	■	■	■	■	■	■				■			■					■	■
West Virginia		■	■	■	■	■	■	■					■							■		
Wisconsin						■																
Wyoming						■																
Total	1	28	28	27	21	34	26	27	20	2	4	5	19	7	7	5	1	1	1	1	1	12

U.S. TERRITORIES

	No Info.	Capital	Robbery/Burglary	Sex Crime	Kidnap	Felony	Weapons	Assault & Battery	Drugs	Gangs	Terrorism	Public Offense	Arson	Escape	Vehicular	Schools	Witness	Riot	Shoplifting	Treason	Extortion	Other
Puerto Rico						■																

CANADA

	No Info.	Capital	Robbery/Burglary	Sex Crime	Kidnap	Felony	Weapons	Assault & Battery	Drugs	Gangs	Terrorism	Public Offense	Arson	Escape	Vehicular	Schools	Witness	Riot	Shoplifting	Treason	Extortion	Other
B. Columbia		■		■																		
Manitoba		■	■				■	■					■	■								
New Brunswick		■		■																		
New Foundland	■																					
Nova Scotia		■		■																		
Ontario		■		■																		
Quebec		■		■			■	■				■		■								
Yukon		■		■																		
Total	1	7	1	6			2	2				1	1	2								

39

TABLE 1.5
Offenses for Which Juveniles Could Be Transferred to Adult Jurisdictions

	No Info.	Capital Offense	Robbery & Burglary	Sex Crime	Kidnap	Felony	Weapons	Assault & Battery	Drugs	Gangs	Terrorism	Public Offenses	Arson	Escape	Vehicular	Witness	Riot	Other	Total
UNITED STATES																			
Alaska		3	13	1	2	2													21
Alabama	■																		305
Arkansas	■																		
California		60	207	7	5		3	74	27				1	1	2			8	395
Colorado		14					4											5	23
Connecticut	■																		2,022*
Delaware	■																		
Florida	■																		4,982*
Georgia		13	35	6		4	1	11	1									5	76
Hawaii	■																		
Idaho	■																		35
Illinois	■																		
Indiana		8				72												1	81
Iowa	■																		23
Kansas				1					3									31	35
Louisiana		62	67	13			1	2	2									1	148
Maryland	■																		
Michigan		26	34						4									90	154
Minnesota	■																		21
Mississippi		22	79	7		4		18	6				1					10	147
Nebraska		6	49	8		9	3	7	8		1	2		3				3	99
Nevada				1		38			1									1	41
New Mexico	■																		49
New York	■																		195
N. Carolina																			3,101
N. Dakota																			6
Ohio	■																		119
Oklahoma		8	35	4			1	4	9					2	2			7	72

* Data represent juveniles 21 and under.

	No Info.	Capital Offense	Robbery & Burglary	Sex Crime	Kidnap	Felony	Weapons	Assault & Battery	Drugs	Gangs	Terrorism	Public Offenses	Arson	Escape	Vehicular	Witness	Riot	Other	Total
Oregon		3	9			1		5										2	20
Pennsylvania		26	20	1				14	9									5	75
S. Carolina	■																		
S. Dakota			1	2			2							1					6
Tennessee		15	22	1		2	2												42
Texas			16	9				196	13									16	250
Utah		3	8	1		1	6	1					1	1		1	2	1	26
Virginia		121	140	33	37	8		42	26			2						6	415*
Washington	■																		95
W. Virginia	■																		5
Wisconsin	■																		139
Wyoming	■																		20
Total	19	390	735	95	44	127	25	385	108	2	1	4	3	8	4	1	2	192	13,243

U.S. TERRITORIES

	No Info.	Capital Offense	Robbery & Burglary	Sex Crime	Kidnap	Felony	Weapons	Assault & Battery	Drugs	Gangs	Terrorism	Public Offenses	Arson	Escape	Vehicular	Witness	Riot	Other	Total
Puerto Rico	■																		

CANADA

	No Info.	Capital Offense	Robbery & Burglary	Sex Crime	Kidnap	Felony	Weapons	Assault & Battery	Drugs	Gangs	Terrorism	Public Offenses	Arson	Escape	Vehicular	Witness	Riot	Other	Total
B. Columbia	■																		5
Manitoba		3	1			1		3					1	1					10
New Brunswick	■																		19
New Foundland	■																		
Nova Scotia																			
Ontario	■																		
Quebec	■																		
Yukon	■																		
Total	6	3	1			1		3					1	1					34

TABLE 1.6
Gender and Race of Juveniles Held as Adults in 1996

	No Info.	Male	Female	White	Black	Native Am./ Aboriginal	Asian	Hispanic	Other	Total
UNITED STATES										
Alaska		21		9	5	5		2		21
Alabama		298	7	74	230				1	305
Arkansas	■									
California		391	4	40	134			191	30	395
Colorado		20	3	3	7	1	1	11		23
Connecticut		*	*	120	437		3	293		2,022*
Delaware	■									
Florida		4,622	349	2,146	2,775				61	4,982**
Georgia		75	1	9					67	76
Hawaii	■									
Idaho		34	1							35
Illinois	■									
Indiana		76	5	31	42			3	5	81
Iowa		22	1	*	*	*	*	*	*	23
Kansas		34	1	12	21	1		1		35
Kentucky	■									2
Louisiana		141	7	18	130					148**
Maryland	■									
Michigan		153	1	41	103				10	154
Minnesota	■									21
Mississippi		140	7	16	130		1			147
Nebraska		97	2	48	24	10	2	15		99
Nevada		41	0	8	17	2	3	11		41
New Mexico	■									49
New York		188	7	*	*	*	*	*	*	195
N. Carolina				747	2,267	51	12		24	3,101**
N. Dakota	■									6

* No information provided in this category. Thus, the totals of individual columns may not equal totals on right.

** Data represent juveniles 21 and under.

	No Info.	Male	Female	White	Black	Native Am./ Aboriginal	Asian	Hispanic	Other	Total
Ohio		117	2	*	*	*	*	* *	11	119
Oklahoma		71	1	28	32	6		6		72
Oregon		20		4	8	0	1	7		20
Pennsylvania		75		10	57	0		8		75
S. Carolina	■									
S. Dakota		6		1		5				6
Tennessee		41	1	4	38					42
Texas		240	10	34	130			83	3	250
Utah		26		10	1	1	2	10	2	26
Virginia		413	2	63	349			3		415**
Washington		88	7	*	*	*	*	*	*	95
West Virginia		*	*	*	*	*	*	*	*	5
Wisconsin		*	*	*	*	*	*	*	*	139
Wyoming		18	2	14		1	1	4		20
Total	8	7,468	421	3,490	6,937	83	26	648	214	13,245

U. S. TERRITORIES

	No Info.	Male	Female	White	Black	Native Am./ Aboriginal	Asian	Hispanic	Other	Total
Puerto Rico	■									

CANADA

	No Info.	Male	Female	White	Black	Native Am./ Aboriginal	Asian	Hispanic	Other	Total
B. Columbia	■					5				5
Manitoba		8	2			9			1	10
New Brunswick		17	2	15		1			3	19
New Foundland	■									
Nova Scotia	■									
Ontario	■									
Quebec	■									
Yukon	■									
Total	6	25	4	15		10			4	34

TABLE 1.7
Gender and Race of Juveniles Held as Adults (Aggregated) in 1996

	No Info.	Black		White		Native Am./ Aboriginal		Hispanic		Asian		Other		Total
		M	F	M	F	M	F	M	F	M	F	M	F	
UNITED STATES														
Alaska		5	0	9	0	5	0	2	0	0	0	0	0	21
Alabama		224	6	73	1	0	0	0	0	0	0	1	0	305
Arkansas	■													
California		134	40	0				189	2			29	1	395
Colorado	■													23
Connecticut	■													2,022*
Delaware	■													
Florida	■													4,982*
Georgia				9								66	1	76
Hawaii	■													
Idaho	■													35
Illinois	■													
Indiana	■													81
Iowa	■													23
Kansas		20	1	12	0	1	0	1	0	0	0	0	0	35
Kentucky	■													2
Louisiana		125	5	16	2									148*
Maryland	■													
Michigan		102	1	41	0							10		154
Minnesota		10		7		1						3		21
Mississippi		124	6	15	1					1				147
Nebraska	■													99
Nevada		17	0	8	0	2	0	11	0	3	0			41
New Mexico	■													49
New York	■													195
N. Carolina	■													3,101*
N. Dakota	■													6
Ohio	■													119

* Data represent juveniles 21 and younger.

	No Info.	Black		White		Native Am./ Aboriginal		Hispanic		Asian		Other		Total
		M	F	M	F	M	F	M	F	M	F	M	F	
Oklahoma		32	0	27	1	6	0	6	0					72
Oregon		4	0	8	0	0	0	7	0	1	0	0	0	20
Pennsylvania		57	0	10	0	0	0	8	0	0	0	0	0	75
S. Carolina	■													
S. Dakota		0	0	1	0	5	0	0	0	0	0	0	0	6
Tennessee		38	4											42
Texas	■													250
Utah		1	0	10	0	1	0	10	0	2	0	2	0	26
Virginia	■													415*
Washington	■													95
West Virginia	■													5
Wisconsin	■													139
Wyoming		0	0	12	2	1	0	4	0	1	0			20
Total	**24**	**891**	**63**	**258**	**7**	**22**	**0**	**238**	**2**	**8**	**0**	**111**	**2**	**13,245**

U.S. TERRITORIES

	No Info.													
Puerto Rico	■													

CANADA

	No Info.													Total
B. Columbia	■													5
Manitoba	■													10
New Brunswick	■													19
New Foundland	■													
Nova Scotia														0
Ontario	■													
Quebec	■													
Yukon	■													
Total	**7**													**34**

TABLE 1.8
Housing of Young Offenders

	No Info.	Juvenile Facility	Adult Facility	Federal Law	Private	Separate	Classified	Temporary
UNITED STATES								
Alaska	■							
Alabama		■						
Arkansas	■							
California		■	■					
Colorado		■	■					
Connecticut		■	■			■		
Delaware			■					
Florida			■			■		
Georgia		■	■			■		
Hawaii	■							
Idaho	■							
Illinois		■			■			
Indiana			■					
Iowa		■	■				■	
Kansas		■	■			■		
Louisiana		■	■				■	■
Maryland			■				■	■
Michigan		■	■				■	
Minnesota			■				■	
Mississippi	■		■					
Nebraska		■	■			■		
Nevada			■					
New Mexico		■		■		■		
New York		■	■			■		■
N. Carolina		■					■	
N. Dakota	■							
Ohio		■	■			■	■	■
Oklahoma		■	■			■	■	■

	No Info	Juvenile Facility	Adult Facility	Federal Law	Private	Separate	Classified	Temporary
Oregon		■			■		■	
Pennsylvania		■		■				
S. Carolina		■	■				■	
S. Dakota			■					
Tennessee			■			■		
Texas				■		■		
Utah			■				■	
Virginia		■	■				■	
Washington			■				■	
West Virginia		■				■		■
Wisconsin		■	■			■		
Wyoming		■						
Total	6	23	26	3	2	13	13	6

U.S. TERRITORIES

	No Info	Juvenile Facility	Adult Facility	Federal Law	Private	Separate	Classified	Temporary
Puerto Rico		■		■		■		

CANADA

	No Info	Juvenile Facility	Adult Facility	Federal Law	Private	Separate	Classified	Temporary
B. Columbia		■	■	■		■		
Manitoba		■	■	■		■		
New Brunswick		■	■	■		■		■
New Foundland	■							
Nova Scotia		■	■	■		■		
Ontario		■	■	■		■		■
Quebec		■	■	■		■		■
Yukon		■	■	■		■		■
Total	1	7	7	7		7		4

TABLE 1.9
Problems and Issues Arising from Juveniles in Adult Facilities

	No Info.	Gangs	Safety	Rape	Classification	Separation	Federal Law	Escape	Program	Survival	Transition	Lack of Education	Social Skills	Attention	Behavior	Suicide
UNITED STATES																
Alaska	■															
Alabama	■															
Arkansas	■															
California	■															
Colorado		■														
Connecticut	■															
Delaware	■															
Florida	■															
Georgia	■															
Hawaii	■															
Idaho	■															
Illinois	■															
Indiana	■															
Iowa			■													
Kansa	■															
Louisiana	■															
Maryland			■	■	■	■										
Michigan			■		■	■										
Minnesota	■															
Mississippi	■															
Nebraska								■								
Nevada	■															
New Mexico	■															
New York	■															
N. Carolina	■															
N. Dakota	■															
Ohio	■															
Oklahoma	■															

	No Info.	Gangs	Safety	Rape	Classification	Separation	Federal Law	Escape	Program	Survival	Transition	Lack of Education	Social Skills	Attention	Behavior	Suicide
Oregon	■															
Pennsylvania	■															
S. Carolina	■															
S. Dakota	■															
Tennessee	■															
Texas		■														
Utah		■	■		■	■			■	■						
Virgina	■															
Washington		■	■	■						■	■	■	■	■		
West Virginia	■															
Wisconsin	■															
Wyoming	■															
Total	**32**	**4**	**5**	**2**	**3**	**3**	**0**	**1**	**1**	**2**	**1**	**1**	**1**	**1**	**0**	**0**

U.S. TERRITORIES

	No Info.	Gangs	Safety	Rape	Classification	Separation	Federal Law	Escape	Program	Survival	Transition	Lack of Education	Social Skills	Attention	Behavior	Suicide
Puerto Rico													■			

CANADA

	No Info.
B. Columbia	■
Manitoba	■
New Brunswick	■
New Foundland	■
Nova Scotia	■
Ontario	■
Quebec	■
Yukon	■
Total	**8**

TABLE 1.10
Programs for Juveniles in Adult Facilities

	No Info.	No Program	Basic Education	Vocational Education	Computers	Religious	Self-Help	Job Training	Boot Camp	Alcohol/Drug Abuse	Anger	Individual	Sex Offense	Cognitive Reasoning	Special Education	Gangs	AIDS Education	Relapse	Parenting	Victim Awareness	Wellness	Separate Program	Transition	Pre-Release	Suicide
UNITED STATES																									
Alaska		■																							
Alabama			■	■																					
Arkansas	■																								
California			■	■	■	■	■	■	■		■	■													
Colorado			■	■			■	■		■		■			■	■	■	■							
Connecticut			■	■	■	■	■	■	■	■	■	■	■		■	■	■	■	■	■			■	■	
Delaware	■																								
Florida	■																								
Georgia			■	■		■	■			■	■	■		■						■	■				
Hawaii	■																								
Idaho		■																							
Illinois		■																							
Indiana		■																							
Iowa	■																								
Kansas																					■				
Louisiana														■											
Maryland	■																								
Michigan			■	■	■				■			■		■											
Minnesota		■																							
Mississippi	■																								
Nebraska			■	■					■																
Nevada		■																							
New Mexico		■																							
New York			■	■		■	■		■	■						■		■					■	■	
N. Carolina			■	■					■	■	■	■													
N. Dakota		■																							
Ohio		■																							
Oklahoma	■																								

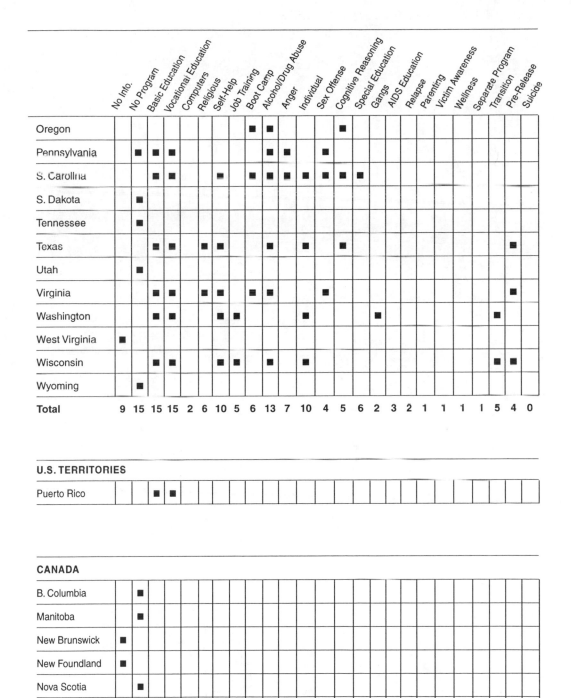

	No Info.	No Program	Basic Education	Vocational Education	Computers	Religious	Self-Help	Job Training	Boot Camp	Alcohol/Drug Abuse	Anger	Individual	Sex Offense	Cognitive Reasoning	Special Education	Gangs	AIDS Education	Relapse	Parenting	Victim Awareness	Wellness	Separate Program	Transition	Pre-Release	Suicide
Oregon								■	■					■											
Pennsylvania		■	■	■					■	■			■												
S. Carolina			■	■			■		■	■	■	■		■	■	■									
S. Dakota		■																							
Tennessee		■																							
Texas			■	■		■	■			■		■		■										■	
Utah		■																							
Virginia			■	■		■	■	■	■				■											■	
Washington			■	■			■	■				■				■							■		
West Virginia	■																								
Wisconsin			■	■			■	■		■		■											■	■	
Wyoming		■																							
Total	**9**	**15**	**15**	**15**	**2**	**6**	**10**	**5**	**6**	**13**	**7**	**10**	**4**	**5**	**6**	**2**	**3**	**2**	**1**	**1**	**1**	**1**	**5**	**4**	**0**

U.S. TERRITORIES

	No Info.	No Program	Basic Education	Vocational Education	Computers																				
Puerto Rico			■	■																					

CANADA

	No Info.	No Program
B. Columbia		■
Manitoba		■
New Brunswick	■	
New Foundland	■	
Nova Scotia		■
Ontario		■
Quebec	■	
Yukon		■
Total	**3**	**5**

2 Adolescent Development

Background

We now turn to a discussion of adolescent development. We already have provided a history of the juvenile and adult corrections systems in Section One. We followed juveniles in a variety of settings and reviewed how society attempted to hold criminals, no matter what age, accountable for their actions. However, without a context of how the violent youthful offender thinks, perceives, is motivated, and acts, we are destined to repeat history and create, perhaps, a greater problem for ourselves. Indeed, we do have knowledge and experience with the youthful offender and with a greater understanding of adolescent development, we can do better than we now are doing.

This section is devoted to a discussion of the concepts of adolescence and how to apply these concepts in the adult criminal justice systems. Correctional practitioners must have a working knowledge and sound theoretical base for understanding adolescent development if they are to successfully manage, treat, and intervene with the violent young offender in adult correctional programs.

Adolescence is a time of transition from childhood to adulthood, during which the major task of the individual is to establish an adult identity that is fostered through peer group affiliations and positive relationships with adults. The primary task for adolescents is to explore and discover: who they are, what they want to be, what they look like to others, and how to make good decisions.

While many psychologists and other developmental theorists describe adolescence as a life stage of human development, we believe adolescence is a process of growth during which certain attitudes, beliefs, and values are explored, cognitive structuring occurs, and skills are acquired. It is through this process, that the young person has a series of experiences, which lead to greater autonomy and independence. As such, while adolescence may be defined as starting at a particular chronological age, and ending at another, we believe that adolescence is defined by a variety of domains and stages, through which an individual grows and develops.

Indeed, the length of adolescence has increased over the years, such that humans experience a much longer time in adolescence than their counterparts in earlier times. Historically, children were thrust into adult roles much earlier in their chronological development. Years ago, children worked at earlier ages, were forced to participate in social and economic responsibilities at earlier ages, and were not required to participate in

WHAT IS DEVELOPMENT?

Development is the advancement or growth through sequential, progressive changes.

Developmental theory is a series of human growth stages with each stage having certain critical tasks that must be mastered for normal development to occur.

Developmental stage is a chronological period where certain behaviors, experiences, needs, and skills are common and distinguishable from any other age group.

Critical tasks are those emotional, physical, psychological, and social functions that must be mastered so that a person can progress effectively along the continuum of development. As such, there are specific critical tasks which must be mastered and related to each developmental stage.

eductional or developmental tasks as they are today. For example, in 1871, only 5 percent of American youth under the age of eighteen were in high school as compared to 1929, when 33 percent were in high school. In those times, adolescence was considered to begin at thirteen or fourteen, and end by eighteen or nineteen. Today, adolescence is thought to begin as early as ten years of age (or whenever pubescence begins) and extend to twenty-three or twenty-four years of age.

The increase of time during which a human develops through adolescence may be due to a variety of reasons. Most common include such changes in American society as:

- Enactment of compulsory education laws
- Establishment of a juvenile or family court system
- Requirements of the labor market for more education and training
- Children are no longer needed to support the family economically
- Enactment of child labor laws to protect children from being exploited in factories and other work situations
- Decrease in the number of children in a family
- Child advocates and child protective laws became more vigilant

Beyond the societal issues that may have had an impact on adolescent development, other circumstances need to be considered. We have noted that today humans begin adolescence at an earlier chronological age. As science has developed more sophisticated medical practices, keeping children healthier, with better medicines and nutrition, humans have developed physically and mentally at earlier chronological ages. With more families requiring both parents to work, the social and emotional requirements for children to mature earlier has increased, which also lowers the age at which adolescence begins. So too, humans are exposed to situations on television and other media that provide them with information and insights which in previous generations were unavailable until later in their chronological development. With the advent of a more advanced technical society, children are required to spend more time in formal education; with the reduction in low-skilled jobs, more training and experience is necessary; with the social value of delaying marriage and childbearing, fewer individuals leave their nuclear families to live on their own at adolescence. All of these factors have contributed to a longer period of adolescent development.

Normal Development

Adolescence consists of three phases:
1. Early adolescence, which is approximately from ages eleven to fourteen
2. Middle adolescence, which is approximately from ages fifteen to seventeen
3. Late adolescence, which is approximately from ages eighteen through the early twenties

Within these phases, various actions, behaviors, and processes occur. For adults to competently manage this group, they must be able to understand these actions, behaviors and processes. As a start, they should view and interpret (violent youthful offender) behavior in four critical domains: physical development, cognitive development, emotional development, and social development.

Physical Development

Adolescence is a time of drastic and dramatic physical change. During early adolescence, the young person's body appearance changes. Hair begins to grow and become darker under the arms, around the genitals, legs, and arms. The genitalia in males become larger, and females generally begin menses. Also, in early adolescence, the individual may experience tremendous growth spurts. A young boy or girl may grow from two-to-four inches within a three-month time period. As such, there may be much physical discomfort, especially in the joints such as the knees, ankles, and wrists. There also are changes in the individual's hormones (substances produced by one organ and conveyed to another which is stimulated by the substance's chemistry), particularly the sex hormones of testosterone and progesterone. These changes produce a variety of physical and emotional reactions that may create extreme moodiness and impulsivity. By the onset of middle adolescence, the individuals, because of their physical development, have a greater need for privacy and alone time. (Now, as a corrections practitioner, imagine placing a young offender in a cell block with little or no privacy; or dealing with acting out and impulsive behavior driven by chemical changes.)

Cognitive Development

The physical changes that occur in the brain during adolescence along with educational and social experiences, are some of the factors that account for how adolescents think differently from their younger counterparts. During early adolescence, there is a strong emphasis on the "here and now," with an initial change from concrete to more abstract thinking. During this time, early adolescents begin to make plans, learn to consider alternatives, monitor themselves, and practice making inferences and generalizations. This is why so many adults have difficulty and are frustrated when young people in this phase of development constantly try different plans and always seem to change their minds in pursuing a particular goal. During this period, young people explore different career options and fantasize about future occupations (no matter how unrealistic).

During middle adolescence, young people develop the ability to think abstractly. They now are able to consider possibilities, think about ideal situations (the ideal parent, mate, society, boss), and imagine what could be rather than what is currently. Adolescents, in this phase, are able to connect concepts and draw connections between ideas. During this time, young people engage in self-talk, actively thinking through situations in their own minds through internal conversations, and actively develop an ability to think about their own thinking (this is known as metacognition). Interests and skills are further defined as the adolescent develops specific subject area competencies in school and develops career awareness through exploration and preparation (such as in after-school jobs).

By late adolescence, cognitive development already has survived school transitions such as elementary to middle school, and from middle to high school. Young people in this phase of development also have acquired the necessary skills for postsecondary education or skilled employment. Late adolescents have developed mature thought processes including: making generalizations, engaging in inferential thinking (reading between the lines), and making career and/or vocational decisions.

Emotional Development

Perhaps, one of the most misunderstood domains about adolescents is their emotional growth. What caregivers often experience is a roller coaster ride of mood swings from extreme withdrawal to animated hyperactivity. One moment the young person may be hysterical in laughter, the next hysterical in tears. In the morning, a young person may be daring and challenging, and by bedtime, that same individual may be curled in a fetal position in bed weeping and intimidated. As caregivers, having a paradigm with which to approach adolescents in their emotional upheaval is critically important. Understanding this paradigm is even more helpful when, as corrections staff, we are required to provide a safe and secure environment for all offenders in our charge.

There is a propensity for adolescents to be egocentric. However, during early adolescence, there is an extreme preoccupation with self. Those in early adolescence tend to think that everyone is looking at them and thinking about them. There is paranoia about what they are doing and who is making statements about them. During this phase of adolescence, the young person begins to pull away from the family and seek validation from friends and peer groups.

Role models and heroes become influential during middle adolescence. Young people in middle adolescence begin to look for role models in the media, especially television. While in school and in the community, the young adolescent will tend to identify those peers who they can emulate. During this time period, middle adolescents further explore their selfhood and identity. It is not uncommon to see young people in this phase of development experimenting with their hair and clothes. Green hair, purple hair, streaked hair, baggy jeans, colorful shirts and hats, are all props that young persons use as they begin to firm up their identity. Also note, middle adolescents also experiment with the music they listen to as well as the interests and activities in which they participate.

By the time individuals reach late adolescence, they make decisions relative to their own identity. Peer influences now take precedence over family. In fact, the role of the family in the young person's decision making is quite diminished. This creates some dissonance for the late adolescent for the family remains the most important force in the emotional development of human beings. What happens within the family unit either may lead to emotionally healthy adults or erect roadblocks that create tremendous problems for individuals to resolve. Typically, during early adolescence, there is a growing friction between children and parents, especially as the roles and expectations of each begin to change. During middle adolescence, teens want more privacy at home and develop active emotional ties with peers outside the home and away from the family. As late adolescence is negotiated, young people begin to reintegrate with their family as adults, acting and behaving in a mature role.

Social Development

One of the hardest behaviors to understand in adolescent development is the social interactions of young people as they complete their task to formulate a healthy, law-abiding self identity. Beginning in early adolescence, young persons spend more than half their time with peers and only 15 percent of their time with their families. For the early adolescent, belonging to a clique or group becomes most important. During this time, young people are most vulnerable to gang influences. Since during this phase of adolescence, a great deal of time is devoted to social relationships, the early adolescent is most interested in same-sex cliques and social groups. While dating begins at this time, this social interaction is secondary to other issues. Some of these include experimenting with drugs, drinking alcohol, and investigating sexual activities and relationships.

Since popularity is defined by the activities in which the adolescent participates, individuals in this early stage of adolescence tend to base their decisions on and characterize each other on rather superficial criteria.

By middle adolescence, individuals usually engage in male-female activities, such as dating and active sexual relationships. Friendships become more mature and are based on internal emotional principles such as empathy, trust, self-disclosure, and loyalty. There is an ability to develop intimacy and love relationships during this stage. Most individuals, by the time they complete middle adolescence, also develop a tolerance of individual differences. Late adolescents transition from group affiliation to specific one-on-one relationships. By the end of high school, most adolescents have experimented with drugs and or alcohol, and 50 percent of these late adolescents are sexually active (U.S. Department of Health and Human Services, 1997).

Adolescents' primary concern is to identify who they are and what they are able to do, so that they can take their place in the world. As such, our efforts as adult corrections staff who interact with adolescents is to help them in that mission. The programs we design and implement should aid the adolescent growth process supporting adolescents' cognitive, social, emotional, and physical development. Integrating these areas insures competent, prosocially skilled adolescents.

Aggression, Violence, and the Development of Antisocial Behavior

We live in a violent and hostile world, where young people learn at a very early age that aggression pays. Aggression is *richly, immediately, effectively, and efficiently rewarded.* Aggression is taught in our homes, our schools, and our communities; and it is taught better than we teach our young people to read and write or be constructive, prosocial citizens.

From a historical perspective, Table 2.1 supports our conviction that aggression pays, and our young people learn to be violent and hostile at a very early age. In 1978, juvenile arrests had grown by over 300 percent since 1974, according to the Federal Bureau of Investigation *Uniform Crime Reports*. Even though juveniles comprised only 20 percent of the population then, they accounted for 43 percent of the arrests. Note what happened to juvenile crime rates from 1975-1978, over a three-year time period. Robberies increased by 376 percent; aggravated assaults grew by almost 250 percent; and the absolute number of youth arrested for violent juvenile crimes under the age of eighteen was well over two million.

Another study was conducted by Senator Birch Bayh, the chairman of the Senate Education Committee in 1974. As indicated in Table 2.2, Bayh surveyed 750 school districts throughout the United States, over 84,000 schools within a three-year time span. Bayh reported increases in youth

TABLE 2.1

Juvenile Arrests and Crime Incidents according to the FBI from 1975-1978

Crime	Percentage Increase
Total Arrests	300
Robbery	376
Aggravated Assault	249
Homicide	211

Source: Federal Bureau of Investigation, 1974, *Uniform Crime Reports*

violence within these schools occurring at astronomical proportions: Homicides increased by 18 percent; rapes and attempted rapes were increasing by over 40 percent; robberies increased by 37 percent. However, take special note of the assaults on students and the assaults on teachers—each increased by 85 percent and 77 percent, respectively. Students were becoming more aggressive and violent, indeed. We were beginning to see, even back then, a pattern where students in schools became more brazen in their actions. No longer were crimes committed only against property—now, young people were taking actions against people, another indication that they were becoming more virulent in their aggressive behaviors.

TABLE 2.2
School Safety Survey

The Safe School Study of 1975, surveyed 750 school districts, more than 84,000 schools from 1972-1975, and reported increases of violence in the schools:

Percentage Increase 1972-1975	
Homicides	18
Rapes and attempted rape	40
Robberies	37
Assaults on students	85
Assaults on teachers	77
Burglaries	12
Weapons confiscated	54

Goldstein and Glick (1987) and Glick (1979), who developed Aggression Replacement Training for aggressive adolescents, began studying these and other data on violent and aggressive behaviors in adolescents. They used their research and experience in an attempt to alert all concerned to a very real problem which, they posited, would only worsen if corrective action were not taken. Our society really has not taken any action to ameliorate these conditions during the last twenty-five years, and the youth violence in our communities only has increased. Young people have become more desensitized to the violence around them, such that they have learned to devalue those they assault, as well as themselves. Indeed, the *FBI Crime Statistics Reports* for the last decade have corroborated the historical data we have provided here.

To further elaborate this point of view, Table 2.3 lists behaviors that were identified in 1940 by school teachers as being inappropriate for their students, resulting in the student being sent to the principal's office (*School Life*, 1962). In contrast, look at what young people are being removed from their classes for now—fifty years later (Goldstein and Glick, 1987). What have we done to so desensitize our children and adolescents to aggression and violence?

TABLE 2.3
School Behavior-Management Problems 1940 Versus 1995

1940	*1995*
Talking out of Turn	Drug Abuse
Chewing Gum	Absentceism
Making Excessive Noise	Alcohol Abuse
Running in School Hallway	Vandalism
Stepping out of Line	Assault
Wearing Improper Clothes	Suicide
Not Putting Wastepaper in Basket	Teenage Pregnancy
	Gambling
	Rape
	Arson

Today, the pattern of violence and adolescent aggressive behavior is becoming even worse. The graphic illustration (see Fig 2.A) demonstrates how violent our society is for our children and young people. One woman is battered every fifteen seconds; one burglary is committed every ten seconds; one robbery occurs every forty-six seconds; one aggravated assault happens every twenty-nine seconds; one violent crime is committed every seventeen seconds; and by the time you finish watching your nightly news hour, approximately three murders will have been perpetrated. We do live in a violent society.

Remember our recurring theme: Aggression is a learned behavior— one that is immediately, effectively, and efficiently and richly rewarded. We teach our young people how to be violent and aggressive in our homes, communities, churches, and schools. We teach them through our newspapers, movies, and television. We teach them by our own actions.

FIGURE 2.A

Time Clock of Violence

One
Violent Crime
Every 17 Seconds

One
Woman Battered
Every 15 Seconds

One
Motor Vehicle Theft
Every 19 Seconds

1.3
Adult Women
Raped Every Minute

One
Robbery
Every 46 Seconds

One
Larceny-Theft
Every 4 Seconds

One
Aggravated Assault
Every 29 Seconds

One
Burglary
Every 10 Seconds

One
Property Crime
Every 2 Seconds

55 Deaths From
Alcohol Related Traffic
Crashes Every Day

One
Murder
Every 21 Minutes

About Six
Children Reported
Abused And Neglected
Every Minute

Source: Bureau of Justice Assistance. 1996. *Fact Sheet*; Civic Research Press. 1997. *Battered Offender Newsletter*; National Institute of Justice. 1996. *Research in Brief*; Office of Juvenile Justice and Delinquency Prevention. 1997. *Fact Sheet, 1996*; ———. 1996. *Combatting Violence and Delinquency: National Juvenile Justice Action Plan.*

In fact, aggression is learned so well by our young people, that they do not even realize how violent they are, to others, and to themselves. They have learned this at a very early age. We, as parents, have taught them. Just think about the following scenario, most familiar to a good number of us:

> Matt and Mary, his younger sister, are in their family room watching television. Mom has just returned from a full day of work and is busy in the kitchen preparing dinner. Matt hits his little sister because she changed the channel he was watching. Upon hearing Mary crying, Mom goes into the family room and asks: "What's going on here?" Mary says: "Matt hit me." At this time, Mom gets angry, bolts over to Matt, and she smacks him several times and states: "Don't you know you are bigger than your sister, and you should not be hitting her!"

What has Matt learned? Effectively and efficiently, Matt has learned that if I am bigger, then I can do what I want to, even hurt you. Our young people learn to be aggressive at tender ages. When parents are busy, where do they usually place their tots to entertain them? Right in front of the television. Television—as we now know because our policymakers have finally begun to talk publicly about it—is one of the primary teachers of aggression and violence for our young people. We know that there are twenty-six acts of violence during one hour of prime time television, when family TV programs are supposed to be aired (National Association Against Media Violence, 1989). These are not just slapstick pokes and jabs, these are assaults and incidents of maiming and murders, where blood and guts are graphically spewed over white walls. Well, how about Saturday morning cartoons? How many acts of violence, actually punching, cutting, shooting, blowing up, and the like, occur on an hour of Saturday morning cartoons? According to the same survey, thirty-seven independent acts of violence occur during one hour of Saturday morning cartoons.

Television violence long has been identified as a cause of aggression among the young. For more than twenty years, organizations of high repute have raised more than passing concern about the amount of violence on the public airways. To wit:

- The American Medical Association passed a resolution in 1976 that states: "Television violence threatens the health and welfare of young Americans."

- The National Institute of Mental Health concluded in 1982 that: "There is a clear consensus among most researchers that television violence leads to aggressive behavior."

- The U.S. Attorney General's Task Force on Family Violence concluded in 1984 that: "The evidence is becoming overwhelming that . . . violence on television . . . may contribute to normal adults and children learning and acting out violent behavior."

- The American Psychiatric Association in 1987 presented testimony to Congress that: "the evidence is overwhelming that violence in television programming can have a negative and severe behavioral impact on young people and adults."
- The American Psychological Association concluded in 1992 that: ". . . viewing televised violence may lead to increases in aggressive attitudes, values, and behavior, particularly in children."

What further evidence do we need that children are desensitized to the violence around them at a very early age. They learn in their homes from their parents, on television, and from their friends, that aggression pays; it is immediately and effectively rewarded.

Unfortunately, we now know from literally hundreds of studies conducted on aggressive and violent young children that certain patterns and conditions promote aggression in young people. There are several broad categories that foster aggression which include:

- **Weak familial or social bonding**. If children do not have family, friends, or other appropriate social support systems, they will compensate through behaviors they see elsewhere, that is on television and in the movies.

- **Aggressive young people are frequently the targets of aggression themselves.** They are the Matts and Marys of the world who have been abused by their parents or bullied by their brothers and sisters, or beaten by their peers.

- **Aggressive children and adolescents frequently see violent and aggressive acts perpetrated with successful, immediate, effective rewards.** If I want something, such as your pen, and I take it with no consequence for my action, those who witness that act get a clear message that aggression pays. There is little disincentive to stop those witnessing aggression from becoming aggressors themselves.

- **Aggressive children and adolescents are also favorably and richly rewarded for their own aggressive behaviors**. Specifically, once aggression is attempted with success, the tendency to repeat that action increases and is self-reinforcing.

- **Aggressive young people are deficient in moral reasoning**. We know from research (Goldstein and Glick, 1987, 1989, 1994) that aggressive and violent adolescents do not view their world in a fair, just, and equitable manner.

- **Violent and aggressive young people do not have appropriate prosocial skills.** We also know from research (Goldstein and Glick, 1987, 1989, 1994) that aggressive and violent adolescents lack the necessary social skills with which to negotiate aggressive antisocial situations in which they find themselves.

- **Aggressive young people have information-processing deficits.**
  There is a plethora of educational research, especially in reference
  to the special education population, many of whom are identified as
  "behavior disordered" at very early ages, showing that they have
  problems listening, sitting still, processing information, and following
  instructions. It is these young people who often end up in delinquent
  situations and ultimately in our institutions.

Yet, as corrections staff, we are expected to intervene in these
young persons' lives and insure some change in their behaviors before
they are returned to society. Therefore, knowing the concepts of normal
adolescent development, as well as understanding the nature of aggression and how young people develop antisocial behaviors is of great
importance for those who have to manage the violent youthful offender
in adult correctional systems.

Once corrections staff have a thorough understanding of normal adolescent development and the learning of violent behavior, such knowledge
may be used to develop programs within the institution to intervene
successfully in these young people's lives. Consideration of this body of
knowledge may be used to assess the interactions between the staff and
the offender population, which must be served. It may be used to appraise
skill levels of staff in order to decide what may need to be done to enhance
their levels of expertise when they work with this population. Or, the
information may be used to match specific work situations prescriptively
with those young people placed within the institution.

Consider the following to illustrate how critically important it is to
understand and apply the concepts of normal adolescent development.
As a line staff person in an institution (a corrections officer, teacher, or
aide), you are faced with a young offender emotionally acting out. He or
she could be aggressive or just rambunctious. With little or no understanding of the principles of adolescent development, the line staff person
would not know that these behaviors probably are the result of physical
and emotional development of middle adolescence, stemming from an
increased flow of hormones and body changes. As such, the staff reaction
easily could be punitive rather than therapeutic, thus creating a crisis
instead of prescriptively de-escalating the situation using appropriate
adolescent interventions.

3 Organization, Administration, and Management Issues

Until recently, there has been relatively little in the literature that detailed those organizations, administrations, and management concerns needed to implement criminal justice programs. Glick (1983, 1986) identified some elements that were reliably successful for juvenile justice programs. Goldstein and Glick (1987) devoted a chapter to administrative principles when they published their cognitive behavioral program for aggressive and violent offenders. More recently, their book *Managing Delinquency Programs that Work* (1995) offered the thoughts of some of the best minds in this field.

This section will concentrate on areas important to the implementation of the programs and services and the overall management of the violent youthful offender in adult corrections systems.

We first explore staff selection and development, and describe those elements necessary to provide the infrastructure required for sound, effective, and efficient programs. We next focus on classification and needs assessment, then we present our views of policies and procedures.

We conclude with a discussion of security issues, the foundation upon which any program is developed and implemented.

We advocate that there be a holistic view from the perspective of the violent youthful offenders, with seamless services provided by all staff, both program and security. Though traditionally in separate camps, program staff and security staff do agree, that without a safe and secure environment, program implementation is impossible. At the base of Maslow's Hierarchy of Needs (1954) is physical and psychological safety. He states humans first must satisfy these basic needs before other higher-order needs such as love, belongingness, and esteem may be realized.

Staff Selection and Development

There is a consensus among corrections staff that the violent youthful offender presents special challenges for them. We already have explored those considerations in Sections One and Two, highlighting those areas of adolescent development and aggression of which the adult corrections system needs to be critically aware. There also is agreement among staff, whether they be policymakers, managers, or line staff, that the violent youthful offender requires a special type of corrections staff, one with specific skills and traits needed to work effectively with this population. Corrections systems now encounter many staff who resist working with the violent juvenile offender population. Some reasons that have been identified include, but are not limited to:

- Age differences—some staff believe they are too old; while others are too close in age to the offender
- Lack of respect for the violent youthful offender and inability to change the paradigm that these are "thugs," and or "kids who need to be disciplined"
- Lack of objectivity and a need to form familiar (less than professional) relationships
- Lack of stamina, perseverence, objectivity, consistency, and constancy to deal with adolescents

Staff Selection

In spite of these issues, many systems are enjoined from selecting staff who are most appropriate to serve this violent youthful offender population. Some are required by union contract to post assignments and bid out jobs. As such, many of the youthful offender programs are staffed by the least-senior personnel, both supervisory and direct line staff. Other systems assign staff, who then are unwilling and unable to perform satisfactory jobs for this special population. Often, systems will coerce staff into working in these units by promising that they will rotate out of the unit within thirty to sixty days and, perhaps even their next assignment will be one of their own choice. This strategy often undermines the needs of violent youthful offenders and program integrity, since both require consistency across all variables—including staff. Those staff who volunteer for this type of assignment seem most attractive and successful. In this case, staff seem more motivated, better trained, and ready to expand their own paradigms.

Staff who have special training or education in the area of adolescent development may be better equipped initially to deal with the violent youthful offender. Usually those trained in adolescent theories of treatment approaches have a better sense of the strengths and weaknesses within a program. They also have common baseline knowledge to extend through on-the-job training or by additional professional development opportunities whether they be college courses, professional seminars, or conference sessions. Recruiting security staff for these programs also may be a challenge since many of these staff realize that program staff, such as social workers, work better with this population because they are in contact with them less frequently, about one half hour twice a week; whereas, the security staff are in direct contact with the population eight hours per day, five days per week. Security staff, then, have greater contact for longer periods of time, thus requiring that they receive special training and staff development opportunities.

Staff Qualities

During the past year, we have had exceptional opportunities to speak with a variety of corrections staff, at all levels of operation, from line workers to policymakers, both program and security personnel. Based on our conversations and interviews, we offer the following suggestions to enable staff who work with the violent youthful offender population to be successful:

- **Patience**. Patience has been the number one characteristic/trait identified by every group interviewed. Working with youthful offenders requires a great deal of patience. Unlike their adult counterparts, youthful offenders cling to staff. They require an explanation (as do most adolescents) for every order or request. They question everything they are asked to do and as one group of correctional staff said, "They (youthful offenders) whine more than adults do."

- **Listening Skills**. The youthful offender requires the staff to listen much more than the adult population does. Some staff feel it is because they spend more time with the staff than adults do. "They are talking constantly," one correctional officer said. "Listening to what they have to say gives significant insights into the individual and to the entire youthful offender population as a whole."

- **Attendance**. The youthful offenders need stability in their lives. It is incumbent upon the staff to create and insure that the youth's environment is consistent, constant, safe, and secure. Staff attendance is an important ingredient of that stability. One group of correctional supervisors observed that the youthful offenders know staff's days off, and when someone takes an unscheduled day off, it can be a source of disruption to the stability of the unit and/or activity.

- **Positive Attitude**. Any employee who works with youthful offenders must have a positive attitude and be able to demonstrate that attitude in consistent and predictable behaviors. Youthful offenders, as a rule, have been exposed to a great deal of negativity and look to staff for positive reinforcement in their lives.

- **Team Player**. Agencies find that to work effectively in a youthful offenders' program, staff must be part of an overall team effort. Therefore, being a team player is another characteristic/trait that is necessary for anyone who works with youthful offenders.

- **Physical Ability**. Staff members who work with youthful offenders should have the physical ability to control a youthful offender if they should have to engage in physical confrontation. Also, working with youthful offenders is physically demanding because "they never stop." Correctional officers report that working with youthful offenders requires stamina because they constantly are occupied and actively doing something.

- **Like Teenagers**. The staff members who work with youthful offenders should like teenagers. This sounds like common sense, but adolescents are not little kids. Adolescents can be exasperating just because they are going through normal adolescent development, and staff who work with the violent youthful offender have to accept the fact that these youthful offenders, besides being skill deficient and antisocial, also display typical adolescent behaviors.

- **Two Years of Service**. Correctional officers, staff, and supervisors agree that all staff who work with youthful offenders should have at least two years of corrections service. We believe that a person with two years of experience will have knowledge of the infrastructure of the system, which will enable them to assist the youthful offenders with the issues that arise during their incarceration.

First-line Supervisors and Managers

Just as line staff should possess certain qualities and have basic competencies specific to the youthful offender population, so should the first-line supervisors and managers who must administer the program. It is essential that management staff be selected who have the following traits:

- **Flexibility**. These individuals should have the ability to be flexible both in the supervision of staff and offenders. Managers should be willing to listen to line staff who present new ways of supervising the youthful offenders.

- **Good Communication Skills**. It is important for every supervisor to have good communications skills. It is especially important for those supervisors responsible for youthful offenders. Communicating with adolescents at times can be frustrating and challenging. So, the supervisor must set the example to the staff and offenders on how to communicate effectively with each other.

- **Patience**. Having patience is probably the most important characteristic for a first-line supervisor to have when dealing with youthful offenders. The supervisor must demonstrate restraint in a situation, which is usually intense and challenging.

- **Experience**. The individual should have at least two years as an institutional supervisor. The first-line supervisors have to understand the whole system, so they will be able to integrate the violent youthful offender program in the contextual framework of the entire system.

Adult corrections systems administrators need to change and expand their paradigms as they meet the mandates required of them. Specifically, even though the violent youthful offender seems to be an anomaly in the adult system, the administrators, those who set policy and direct large systemic operations, must be prepared to serve this population, and the staff who must implement it with integrity and vision.

As such, we suggest that administrators be assigned to oversee these youthful violent offender programs who have the following traits:

- **Open paradigms** - Administrators must be willing to listen to the new problems that are associated with incarcerating youthful offenders in adult facilities, at the very least. They must be willing to try new methods and techniques to manage these youthful offenders.

- **Good communicators** - Administrators, as leaders, must have a vision and be able to articulate that vision efficiently and effectively. Administrators must be able to communicate throughout the chain of command and be able to relate issues and concerns about program operations, their staff, and the violent youthful offender population.

- **Experienced** - Administrators must be experienced, and have enough status within the system to be heard when administering the affairs of the program: supervising staff, monitoring programs, managing stakeholder interests, and performing fiscal and budget management.

- **Decision makers** - Because this entire area of incarcerating youthful offenders in adult facilities is so new, the administrators must have the skills and confidence necessary to make decisions where there may not be any precedent, policy, or procedure to follow.

The recruitment and selection of staff is critically important as a fundamental underpinning of any program, but especially for the violent youthful offender programs. Policy stakeholders must ensure that there are adequate staffing levels. This occurs through the recruitment, selection, and retention of well-trained, qualified, and experienced staff. The current paradigm will auger against these parameters, so it will take special staff, from administrators to managers, to supervisors, to line staff who will insure that the program is successful and the violent youthful offenders are well served.

Training

It is imperative that staff be trained to recognize and deal with those issues that are specific to the violent youthful offender population. Just as agencies had to identify and train staff to work with other special needs populations such as the mentally retarded offenders, those in administrative segregation, substance abusers, and sexual offenders, to name but a few, so too, we should train staff to work with youthful offenders.

Ideally, training should take place **before** the correctional staff actually begins to work with the youthful offender population; however, in most cases, that is not practical. What usually happens is that correctional staff already work with youthful offenders and receive their training piecemeal. The more important issue is not how the correctional staff is being trained, but on what they are being trained and the strategies used for the training.

We strongly urge that the cornerstone of youthful offender training should be based on the *stages of adolescent development*. It is critical that correctional staff develop a thorough understanding of each stage of adolescent development because it has such a dramatic impact on all of the issues on which they need to be trained. Staff who appreciate that adolescent development incorporates an understanding of the domains of adolescence that include cognitive, physical, social, and emotional factors, cross tabbed with stages of adolescence (as detailed in Section Two) will be in a better position to intervene appropriately to stop violent youthful offender misbehaviors as they occur. Sometimes, as youthful offenders act out, they do so for other reasons than simply making trouble.

Other courses that we recommend be offered as training for correctional staff who work with violent youthful offenders include:

- **Listening Skills**. Developing active listening skills in staff is an important area of the training. With the youthful offender population, active listening will assist the staff in managing this population. "You really have to listen to these offenders so that you understand what they are saying. They use so much street talk and hide what they really want to say in jargon and verbiage—that many times they are sharing with you something that is very important to them; and if you don't respond to it, they may view your nonresponsive behavior as not caring. All this happens because you didn't initially listen," said one corrections staff member.

- **Conflict Resolution**. A course in nonviolent conflict resolution techniques is essential because the youthful offenders constantly observe how staff deal with conflict. Staff should become masterful at practicing conflict resolution. Conflict resolution also plays an important part in the overall modeling that all staff who work with youthful offenders should display.

- **Role Modeling**. Modeling behavior is a critical skill when working with youthful offenders. For many of these youthful offenders, the correctional staff with whom they come into contact are the only stable adults that they have had in their lives. Correctional staff should understand that one of their primary responsibilities when working with the violent youthful offender is to be an impeccable role model.

- **Self-defense**. A self-defense course should teach a few basic self-defense techniques where mastery of the martial arts techniques is required. Simultaneously, staff also will appreciate that martial arts also require a sense of self-discipline, concentration, obedience to mission, and focus. As such, staff who work with youthful offenders should have the ability to physically control a youthful offender who acts out violently using the minimal amount of force to gain control, effectively, and efficiently.

- **Discipline**. The proper use of the disciplinary system is an essential part of youthful offender management, because the rules and regulations are developed for the adults, not adolescents who are incarcerated. Again, knowing and understanding the stages of adolescent behavior is critically important in discerning what is a rule violation and what is just part of growing up. One facility we visited actually had filled its administrative segregation area with youthful offenders, not because of the seriousness of their offenses, but rather because of the number of their offenses. According to correctional officers interviewed, some of these youthful offenders had received five or six disciplinary write-ups in one day (twenty-four hour period). However, the official disciplinary system only should be used for serious rule violations, and the sanctions should be those geared towards things that youthful offenders do not want to lose such as television privileges, recreation yard, or phone privileges. "Very often they use our own system against us by committing rule violations to fulfill their own needs such as getting a lock-down so that they do not have to go to school, or getting placed in administrative segregation so that they will get a single cell, and also so that they do not have to mix with the rest of the population. They use the system to escape reality. They turn what the system considers a negative into a positive," one manager explained during a recent training session.

- **Paradigms**. Staff should become familiar with what paradigms are and how they can affect our lives. They should acquire an understanding that the paradigms that have been established and recognized as techniques and methods to manage adult inmates often are not as effective with youthful offenders.

- **Security**. Working with youthful offenders brings with it a need to increase security, vigilance, and strict adherence to basic security practices. The staff should be instructed in how to conduct security inspections, pat down searches, contraband control, and escort procedures, so as to assure the basic safety and security of the environment in which these violent youthful offenders must exist.

- **Interpersonal Communication Skills**. Interpersonal communications is another area that must be taught to staff if they are to be successful with the youthful-offender population. Being able to understand how to communicate with adolescents takes specialized training.

- **Recreation.** Staff should be trained in understanding how adolescents recreate and spend their leisure time. It is critically important to be able to supervise youthful offenders both in group and individual activities so that they will use their free time constructively.

Training should not be restricted to just line staff who have direct contact with youthful offenders. Key administrators, managers, and ancillary staff should be trained in the differences between adult and youthful offenders. No doubt, youthful offenders introduce an entirely new dimension to any system. Also, it is important that administrations and ancillary staff are trained to appreciate what the staff have to deal with, when managing youthful offenders.

Some suggested training topics for administrators and ancillary staff include the following:

- **Stages of Adolescent Development**. This is an overview of the stages of adolescent behavior. The goal is to provide an overview but not to have this level of staff develop the in-depth understanding that direct line staff are expected to master.

- **Discipline**. They should develop an awareness of the operational issues that occur when using a disciplinary system that was designed for adults with the violent youthful offender population. This training should emphasize those adolescent stages of development and analyze disciplinary issues and responses in each of the four adolescent growth domains: cognitive, physical, social, and emotional.

- **Paradigms**. Training should be constructed on the fundamental principles that Barker (1993) introduces, challenging administrators and ancillary staff to expand their own paradigms when administering operational and administrative issues.

- **Gangs**. This training should introduce the concepts of power, control, and profit as it impacts on gang operations within the youthful offender program.

Training is a fundamental administrative responsibility to insure effective and efficient program implementation for the violent youthful offender in the adult corrections systems. It is the hallmark of quality operations in which a larger plan for staff development is well articulated. Training and staff development, together, must have support from the chief executive of the system and be available to all staff—line staff, supervisors, managers, administrators, and policymakers, including security and program personnel on a published, well-coordinated schedule.

Classification and Needs Assessment

All systems, adult and juvenile, employ classification and needs assessment strategies to screen and place their offender populations within its institutions and programs. Underlying all of these approaches are principles, which are identified as follows:

- It is important to emphasize that there is no one approach to classify all offenders.

- Each population has different characteristics.

- Each institution has different needs.

- Classification and assessment are not one-time events, but they must be conducted as a continuous process over regular intervals with all offenders.
- Statistical prediction is more accurate than clinical interpretation and prediction.
- Classification decisions based upon objective data, and judgments based on observable behaviors are more reliable, easier to make, more effective, and efficient than those that are not so based.
- Individual decisions, which are based on objective criteria, are less vulnerable to legal challenges.
- Classification of offenders requires decision making. As such, while instruments are used to collect data, people must make decisions to classify offenders.

Travis and Latessa (1996) suggest ten elements of effective classification and assessment. These include:

1. **Purposeful**. Generally, the purpose of classification and assessment is to insure offenders are treated differentially within a system so as to insure safety, adequate treatment, and understanding.

2. **Organizational fit**. We already have discussed elsewhere the idea that organizations and systems have different characteristics, capabilities, and needs. How well does the offender fit within the system and where should the offender be placed are two questions within this principle that need to be explored.

3. **Accuracy**. This element deals with the consistency of the classification and assessment model that is used and how correct the instrument is in placing offenders within the system. Issues of validity and reliability are critical to this element. *Reliability* may be defined as hitting the same spot on a bull's eye target all the time. *Validity* means hitting the bull's eye (center) all the time. If your system is reliable, but not valid, you may be hitting the target consistently, but not the right spot.

4. **Parsimony**. This element concerns some of the basic structure of the classification and assessment systems. How complicated is it to use? How long does it take to administer? What level of expertise and training is required to use the instruments. All of these factors hint at the importance of this element being as simple and concise as possible without violating accuracy.

5. **Distribution**. How well does the classification system differentiate among the offenders. Do all offenders fall in the same category, and how much variation is there? All of these questions are germane to the element of distribution, which insures that the classification of offenders places them in broad categories across the system.

6. **Dynamism**. This has to do with how dynamic or static the methodology is and whether it enhances our decision making. This element is critical to placing the violent juvenile offender in appropriate facilities, but also to identifying programs and services required to meet those needs discussed in Section Two.

7. **Utility**. Classification systems must be useful, and that means that the system must insure its staff understand the system so it is used and implemented, well. Classification systems need to be responsive to the needs of offender, staff, and the organization if they are to be considered useful and have some utility for the corrections system.

8. **Practicality**. A subset, if not a corollary to utility is that the classification system must be practical and must be possible to implement, but it also must make sense to those who use it. While this may seem to be a training issue at first glance, more critically this element suggests that the classification system be practical enough so that it leads to better decision making when it comes to placing and serving the violent youthful offender.

9. **Justice**. The decisions made as a result of the classification system must be just and consistent. As such, offender placement and service provision should be based upon youthful offender differences, those that are real, measurable, and yield consistent outcomes, regardless of subjective impressions.

10. **Sensitivity**. This element is as much a goal of the classification paradigm, as it is an element of it. The classification process should be sensitive to the differences of offenders. As such, a classification and needs assessment system for youthful offenders should take into account those critical tasks that the offender exhibits (over the four domains of adolescence—physical, cognitive, social, and emotional and the stage of adolescence of that offender).

Penal classification systems are designed to support (1) managing the risk to security, custody, or program disruption, (2) planning for more effective interventions to reduce probabilities of reoffending in the future, (3) managing the risk of recidivism during supervision, and (4) using correctional resources more efficiently. Indeed, while most correctional systems embrace all of these goals in their classification systems, none of these actually speak to the needs of the youthful offender.

In our work with jurisdictions across the country, we constantly are reminded that most adult systems were of the opinion that they merely could extend their current systems and apply each to the violent youthful offender they now were incarcerating. The awakening that they cannot do so is earth shattering—administrators realize that youthful offenders, while they have committed some heinous acts, are still youth, who are in the middle of their adolescent development. Therefore, we must stretch our paradigms yet further to include some of the needs this younger population now present. As such, many of our classification systems will have to be retooled and reengineered, to best meet the needs of the adolescent, as discussed earlier.

Practically, the corrections systems will have to use those elements and principles we have described in this section and apply these to the adolescent now incarcerated. More importantly, the staff assigned to this program will have to be excellent observers of behavior and trained to document what they see, so that they can inform the classification system and change it, accordingly. Only then will the integrity, practicality, and utility of the system be maintained and applied to the challenge of the violent youthful offender.

Policies and Procedures

The advent of youthful offenders in adult corrections facilities creates a need to review existing policies and procedures and develop new policies and procedures. We believe that nowhere else in corrections is the development and review of policies and procedures more important than it is for the violent youthful offender now adjudicated and placed in adult corrections systems. Once policies and procedures are written, it is incumbent upon the system to insure that they are implemented as developed.

Although society wants youthful offenders sent to adult prisons to be punished for their transgressions, it does not want them mistreated and/or injured in any way while they are in prison. When a serious incident happens that involves a youthful offender, the policies and procedures governing the circumstances of that situation will be scrutinized closely. The lack of policies and procedures that currently exist which address the issues of the care, custody, administration, and operations for youthful offenders underscores our concern. During the last several years in which we have consulted for jurisdictions responsible for the violent youthful offender, we have found a paucity of relevant policies and procedures and a rush to develop these. In effect, our corrections system is playing catch up to meet the legislative and executive mandate now foisted upon them.

As agencies embark on developing policies and procedures to deal with youthful offenders, there are issues which they find unique to this population. Unlike their adult counterparts, the entire issue of incarcerating youthful offenders in adult facilities has many ambiguous areas. These create serious difficulties for policy developers and decision makers.

For example, some policy decisions include: Should youthful offenders be examined by a pediatrician? If yes, how often; if no, why not? Can tobacco products be sold to youthful offenders? Does the correctional system have to provide the same educational opportunities as required by law for any youth under the age of sixteen? If a youthful offender is identified as in need of special education and has received such services, must the corrections system comply with the existing requirements and provide those same services while the youth is incarcerated? Is the corrections system under the same mandates relative to the Child Protective Services Act? If so, does the facility have to provide the toll free number to the violent youthful offender population and others mandated to report child abuse?

As with any policy and procedure development, there are some specific sources that should be researched as the policies and procedures are developed. Federal and state laws, codes and industry standards all will provide material that could or, in some cases, must be incorporated in the corrections system's policies and procedures. (For example federal child labor laws restrict those under the age of sixteen from working in certain areas and from using power machinery and equipment.)

We suggest that to begin the process to ascertain what policies and procedures are needed to accommodate the youthful offender population, administrators first review current policies and procedures to discern what is already in place and applicable. Beware, do not assume that your current policies and procedures will be sufficient when dealing with the youthful offender population. Certainly, there are many policies and procedures that are relevant to both adults and youthful offender inmates, but there is also a need to develop policies and procedures specific to the youthful offender population.

Just as specific policies and procedures had to be developed for protective custody and mentally retarded populations because of some unique conditions associated with their confinement, so too there are special conditions for the youthful offender population. It is important that the review of the current policies be systematic and thorough, looking for areas where the treatment of adolescents may differ from that of adults (such as in education and nonemergency medical care, and even job assignments).

We suggest using a team approach to review existing policies and to write new policies and procedures. Representatives from every area concerned with serving the youthful offender should be part of the review team. As such, a staff member from the food service department would be the best person to review and advise about food service policies. That person also would know the other departments with whom food service interacts, and as such, is in the best position to recommend the best interaction and implementation for the policy to be successful.

To illustrate, think of the importance for both the medical and food services areas of consulting with each other and coordinating food service policy development and implementation, especially in the areas of meal planning, setting diet and nutritional goals, and settling on adequate amounts for the youthful offender. There also should be a member of the committee who represents the administration and reports directly to the system's chief executive officer. In this way, those policies and procedures reviewed and/or developed will have direct input from the authority who ultimately approves them.

The team should develop an implementation plan that includes assigning certain policies to specific people to be reviewed within a definite time frame. Written recommendations whether to keep the policy as written or make particular changes to the policy to accommodate youthful offenders should be required of all members. These written statements are useful to establish a paper trail but also are needed for documentation should the team discover that laws or regulations need to be changed and/or clarified, that further legislation is required, and/or that additional resources are needed. The team also should include in their action plan a detailed list of those policies and procedures that need to be reviewed, in priority order, beginning with security, health, and safety issues. The team should specify how the staff will be informed and trained about the changes to the policies and procedures in their action plan. (See Drapkin, 1996, *Developing Policies and Procedures for Jails, A Step-By-Step Guide*, for suggestions on policy development and review.)

Security Issues

"They will test every system we have in place," was a comment from a correctional supervisor when asked how working with youthful offenders affects security operations. To address the security concerns associated with incarcerating youthful offenders in adult facilities, it is important to identify:

- What security systems are currently in place
- How corrections systems inspect and evaluate their programs, services, and institutions
- What measures the systems have written in policy and procedures to protect their staff and their youthful offender population

If we apply the cliche "a chain is only as strong as its weakest link" to the adult corrections system, then we certainly would have to examine closely the area of system and institutional security as the violent youthful offender is placed within the corrections institutions. Corrections managers must insure that the security systems are closely coordinated and integrated into the violent youthful offender paradigm. Toward that end, it is important to consider the following five principles of security for the violent youthful offender:

Principle 1: PEOPLE. This includes those individuals who interact, interface, and communicate to achieve those security requirements/needs necessary for the corrections system to function effectively. This perhaps is the most important principle of the five we discuss in terms of security issues within the system. It is people who implement the program, and it is the staff who create the environment in which the violent youthful offender can participate in a safe and secure program. Security issues depend on a well-trained staff, who are available in sufficient numbers to competently deliver the services required for the youthful offender. With diminishing budgets and greater demand for more efficient operations, security will depend on all staff involved in safety and security issues to work as a team to insure a seamless delivery of services within the corrections environment.

Principle 2: PAPER. This includes those written documents, which clearly articulate the system's position on any given issue that deals with the violent youthful offender. Examples include: policies and procedures, rules and regulations, inspection reports, disciplinary reports, laws, codes, documents generated by the courts, post orders, memoranda, and directives. In fact, the entire security operation should be detailed on paper for it to be an effective mechanism to produce a safe environment for staff and offenders. Documenting and publishing the security system is only one-half of the coin, however. Staff must know what the written documents say, and be able to follow their directives. As such, staff need to be oriented and trained in this entire area, so that when a security incident occurs, whether it be a minor infraction or a major critical incident, there will no surprises that staff were unable to follow direction because they failed to understand the written-paper documentation. The other part of this coin also has to do with the review and constant reevaluation of paper by those staff knowledgeable about the youthful offender. These may include system administrators, managers, first-line supervisors, line staff, as well as citizens who volunteer within the system.

Principle 3: POSTING. This is the deploying of staff to predesignated places so as to perform specific duties and responsibilities, which usually are detailed under Principle 2. Because of the nature of adolescents, even those who are adjudicated youthful violent offenders, there is a need to examine again what the established security posts are and ascertain if the posts still are required or whether there are more productive ways to use the staff assigned to these posts. For example, is there a need to have security staff in the gun towers, or could these security personnel be used more effectively elsewhere? We suggest that systems consider reassigning those staff traditionally assigned to fixed posts such as towers and central services units, to those which are more mobile where staff may supervise the youthful offender more effectively, efficiently, and directly. One system was able to reassign twenty-seven security staff in such a manner to place these individuals where they were sorely needed, in direct contact with the offender in the institution

Principle 4: PLACE. This includes those areas within a correctional environment that require any level of security for any period of time.

Youthful offenders, unlike their adult counterparts, challenge systems to expand their security paradigms when it comes to places whether they be residential, educational, vocational, medical, or dining, to name but a few. Youthful offenders are more active, more impulsive, less thoughtful, and, as such, can create havoc no matter where they may be, unpredictably and without cause. Thus, all areas must be well secured with personnel, lighting, and adequate safeguards. Grates become easy access for escape for the youthful offender, because many of them still are growing and can fit in such spaces. False ceilings, storage containers, lockers (foot and wall), garment storage bags, and other nooks and crannies are all potential security-risk places.

Principle 5: PRODUCTIVITY. This is how efficiently the corrections staff conduct their duties within a specific period of time. Productivity of security staff should be measured by such indicators as: lack of or reduced serious incidents such as fights, suicides, stabbings, and rapes; completion of assigned tasks during each shift; reduction of contraband found in the facility; decrease in property damage; decrease in gang tagging and overt gang activity; and decrease of violations (including contraband) within the secure perimeter of the institution.

One way to integrate these five principles within the security operations of the institution is through security enveloping. Sturgeon, Kerster, and Patrick (1990) define security enveloping as the integrating and interfacing of operations, staff, and facilities, augmented by appropriate technology. We suggest that security enveloping is a way to incarcerate youthful offenders, within our fifth principle of productivity of security systems, because it provides a standardized way to insure security and integrity of the system, thereby increasing its productivity.

Appendix 3 is the Security Envelope Master Checklist. It details those areas to be inspected to evaluate the security levels within an institution. Once accomplished, posting assignments may be developed around the program schedules of the youthful offenders. As a result of the survey, answers to the following questions provide useful information to better plan the offender's day, and thereby the staff's supervisory requirements:

- Where are the offenders coming from and where do they have to go?

- What are the offenders going to use to get where they are going (mode of transportation)?

- What are the security levels of all the areas they are going to pass through and/or enter?

- Will the area that the youthful offenders use need to be searched prior to their arrival and after their departure?

- What will be the duration of time the youthful offenders will spend in the particular place?

The checklist is purposefully detailed and specific to insure adequate security systems and productive staff interaction. We caution, however, that before an institution develops a security envelope, that it conduct a thorough review and audit of the entire facility (or area where the youthful offender will be placed), so that many of the security issues may be identified beforehand.

We conclude this chapter knowing that we have raised more issues than we have answered. However, organization, management, and administration issues are not systemic considerations, that may be treated with a broad brush. While many espouse theory and principles that may be applied generally, the tough issues created by this new breed of corrections' prisoner, the violent youthful offender, must be addressed at the lowest levels of the organizational structure. Thus, jurisdictions, institutions, communities, and those units that can take the specific steps as outlined in this section are urged to do so.

Further, we have highlighted those areas most critical to the management and administration of the violent youthful offender. We next turn to those programs and services, which create the infrastructure, needed to make the changes in these young offenders' lives. We encourage the reader to study carefully some of the more critical interventions that we discuss.

4 Special Needs Populations

Introduction

The challenge for staff to deal with the violent youthful offender in adult correctional systems is difficult enough when one considers and understands the issues of adolescent development theory. Providing adequate services to adolescents is compounded in geometric proportions when the population includes adolescents with special needs. Once correctional professionals learn about the nature and needs of adolescents, these issues provide basic understanding and insight for managing the population, as well as providing foundations for appropriate habilitation and treatment. However, when the population are adolescents who also happen to have special needs, then additional attention must be given to the type of programs offered and services provided. Essentially, the broad interventions usually adapted within the corrections environment are inadequate to meet the requirements of the special-needs offender population. The youthful violent offender requires special services—at the very least. The special-needs violent offender population requires the services and interventions of an informed staff who are able to deal with a variety of different conditions, some caused by the special needs of the offender, some as a result of the offender being an adolescent, and some because the special-needs adolescent happens to be incarcerated.

This section specifically concerns those adolescents who require special attention and highlights: substance abusers, youthful sex offenders, the neglected and sexually and physically abused, as well as those who are suicidal, and those who require special education services. Within each part of this section, we will describe the nature of the special-needs offender and relate this information to adolescent development. Where appropriate, we also will highlight those interventions and services that help the adolescent's positive growth and development, in the hope that all corrections' staff may gain insight into this most challenging offender population.

Substance Abuse

Few would dispute that there is a significant, direct, positive relationship between substance abuse and crime. National Crime Statistics (FBI, 1995) indicate that alcohol was involved in 95 percent of violent crimes on college campuses, and in 90 percent of campus rapes. Alcohol and other substances also were responsible for 42 percent of homicides, 41 percent of assaults, and 36 percent of sexual assaults.

Indeed, substance abuse not only leads to violence and criminal behavior, it is also very expensive. It costs our society 58 billion dollars each year. Two billion dollars are spent on medical costs, 8 billion dollars are estimated to result in lost earnings and other tangible costs, and 48 billion is expended in pain, suffering, and lost quality of life. As a result of these staggering numbers, states have taken action to hold offenders, and especially youthful offenders, accountable for their substance-abusing behaviors, imposing harsh prison sentences for various drug and drug-related crimes. No wonder that nationwide, as much as 62 percent of the incarcerated juveniles are drug involved; and in some states, such as New York, that rate is as high as 72 percent (New York State Division for Youth, 1996).

We also know that substance abuse programs do work. They have an effective impact on criminal behavior. National studies indicate that those aftercare treatment programs that insured abstinence from drugs and alcohol reduced the recidivism rates of offenders (Ohio Department of Alcohol and Drug Addiction Services, 1994). They reduced the number of days offenders were incarcerated (Finigan, 1995) and led to their increased employment (Center for Substance Abuse Treatment,1995). The substance abuse programs that are effective are based on the several program principles, which are discussed in Section Five. Beyond these principles is also the limited risk-control theory posited by O'Leary and Clear (1995). They identify risk management from two perspectives. The first, **risk-controlling factors**, include incarceration and direct supervision. However, risk, according to O'Leary and Clear, also may be managed by **risk-reducing activities**, which are treatment and services provided to the offender while incarcerated or under supervision. As such, these services provide alternatives to just locking offenders away without providing alternative, prosocial skill training.

No matter which program is provided, the corrections staff must begin with the clinical assessments of the offender's needs. These assessments should include information about the following items: history of substance use, and detail about the types and amounts of drugs used; a family history which notes any history of substance abuse; an objective assessment tool which is specific to adolescent substance abusers; a complete social history of the youth; an educational and vocational profile; and current psychological functioning with mental-health status reports, if appropriate. Several states, including Massachusetts, Missouri, and Wisconsin, use specifically designed instruments to assess substance-abuse offenders. The Vermont Risk Need Classification instrument identifies those risk factors, which are statistically related to reoffense if not addressed during the offender's treatment intervention while incarcerated. These factors include substance abuse, emotional stability, employability, and relationships, all of which are the same criminogenic needs identified by Andrews (1990, 1994).

When specifically addressing the youthful violent offender, certain risk factors are more prevalent within these adolescents' backgrounds and need to be specifically addressed with treatment programs. These include:

- Childhood abuse
- Prior history of violence
- Substance abuse
- Impaired mental status
- Demographics such as age, race, and socioeconomic status
- Coming from and going back to high-risk communities that are prone to drugs, violence, and criminality

Finally, when specifically identifying substance abuse among violent youthful offenders, assessments must include those factors that are particular interventions for adolescents. Toward that end, the substance abuse program must be sensitive to and target:

- Specific adolescent stages of development
- Prior history of abuse, substance use, and violence
- Alienation from family and peers
- Perceived power and actual control over one's environment
- Placement of the offender in an appropriate corrections' treatment environment

Substance Abuse Treatment

A Prevention Model for Treatment Intervention

Those who work in the corrections systems would be the first to advocate that prevention is much preferred to a young person being incarcerated, even for a brief period of time. Few would argue that institutionalization is far more expensive than investing in prevention programs. The cost to the taxpayer to incarcerate one substance abuser in prison is approximately $25,000 per year, on the average (Bureau of Justice Statistics, 1996). These same funds, spent in prevention programs, can keep as many as 100 young people from ever using drugs in the first place (DARE Program, 1995).

When we speak of prevention, we often think of the medical field, and inoculating or vaccinating an individual against disease. Yet, in the juvenile and criminal justice systems, prevention often is characterized in three levels: primary prevention, secondary prevention, and tertiary prevention. One may illustrate these concepts in the following manner. Suppose a door-to-door salesman comes home each night, and upon taking off his shoes, finds that there is a hole in his sock. If the man merely discards his socks each night, puts on a new pair the next morning, but upon another day's walking finds another hole in his sock, only to continue putting on a new pair of socks, this is considered **tertiary prevention.** However, if the man decides to darn his socks, only to find that when he put his socks on again, there is a hole from his daily routine, this may be considered **secondary prevention**. It is secondary prevention because he is darning his socks, preventing them from being discarded. If, however, the man inspects his shoes and discovers a small nail in his shoes, removes it and repairs the hole so there is no damage in the first instance, this is **primary prevention**. The salesman has prevented the problem from ever happening.

This prevention model is analogous to adolescent development, specifically for the violent youthful offender. Primary prevention programs are those developmental programs such as the Boy Scouts, Girl Scouts, and 4-H clubs that provide young people with skills and prosocial activities, which give them the appropriate life skills to grow into constructive citizens. Secondary programs are those community-based programs, after school programs, drug programs (such as Alcoholics Anonymous), which support young people who are at risk or at the periphery of the justice system, from becoming more involved in those systems. Tertiary programs are those interventions which habilitate or rehabilitate those offenders already involved in the system. The beauty of this model is that primary, secondary, and tertiary prevention may be applied to any community and system, whether it is a neighborhood or a prison. The corrections system may apply primary, secondary, and tertiary prevention programs even within the prison for the incarcerated youthful offender.

This model may be adapted and applied specifically to substance abuse treatment interventions, providing a structure with which to build a differential and prescriptive system of effective programs and services. No matter what the philosophical premise of the program, or the specific techniques used to effect change, programs may be organized in an array of institutional and community services within the domains of primary, secondary, and tertiary prevention.

Primary Prevention Programs

Primary prevention programs are used with adolescents who have no history of substance use. While most of these programs usually are offered in the community (such as day care centers, schools, churches, or community centers), such programs as Youth Dares, may be appropriate for the 30 percent of the offender population who are not drug involved (Dare Program, 1995). The key to primary prevention programs is that they should be delivered as early as possible in the developmental growth of violent youthful offenders. Even if offenders have committed an act that requires long-term incarceration, but have not been involved with drugs up to that point, prevention programs are appropriate and effective.

Several strategies are employed to effectively implement primary prevention programs. These include:

- **Information dissemination**. This includes providing knowledge and awareness of the nature of drugs and their impact on individuals, families, peers, and communities. Information also should identify resources and provide referrals for additional support. One goal of this strategy is to increase the individual's perceptions of the risk associated with the use of drugs and reinforce a set of values and skills to resist using alcohol, drugs, or other substances abusive to adolescent growth and development.

- **Prevention education**. This is a strategy aimed at teaching critical life and social skills. Such important topics should include critical situational analysis strategies such as forced field analysis, decision making, and refusal skills, to name but a few.

- **Problem identification and referral**. This refers to attempts to identify, educate, and counsel those young offenders who have indulged in age-inappropriate use of drugs, or who have experimented once with drugs. Screening and referral to secondary prevention programs and services are two examples of activities in this area.

Secondary Prevention Programs

Those programs that are considered secondary prevention programs fall into community-based and noncommunity-based (institutional) treatment interventions. When taken together, these programs and services comprise an array of services that are well defined and discrete services provided to the violent juvenile offender who is a drug abuser. The community-based strategies include: *nonintensive services*, which are professionally implemented and require less than nine hours of participation per week, and consist of any combination of individual, group family, and self-help therapies; *intensive services*, which are also professionally implemented and require offenders to participate nine-to-twenty hours per week. In addition to those interventions used in the nonintensive services, these programs also use after school programs, evening programs, and sometimes weekend programs; *day treatment or partial hospitalization* models usually require more than twenty hours per week of participation and are reserved to treat those young people who demonstrate the greatest risk and dysfunction, but not of sufficient nature to require hospitalization.

The noncommunity based strategies include: *medically monitored programs*, which require twenty-four-hour-a-day medical and nursing monitoring, evaluation, and treatment because the offender usually has coexisting medical and/or psychiatric problems and requires between seven-and-forty-five days of residential care. *Medically managed programs* are similar to the medically monitored programs; however, they actually are administered and governed by medical personnel, because the adolescent offender has an acute condition that requires between seven and forty-five days of care. *Intensive residential treatment* is long-term (six-to-twenty-four months) and is directed either professionally or medically, using a therapeutic community model for youth who exhibit multiple problems, including drug and alcohol addictions. *Psychosocial residential treatment* is long term and is designed to provide care to those violent youthful offenders whose disorders do not require intensive residential treatment and are under control with psychotropic and other prescription medicines.

Dealing with Relapse Prevention

Violent youthful offenders within adult systems who are drug users already have demonstrated their addictive behaviors. As in any substance abuse treatment program, juveniles constantly must address those factors that have contributed to their addictive behaviors and consequent antisocial behaviors. As such, institutional programs must address and plan for young offenders to recognize and deal with these addictive behaviors throughout their lives. Such factors as negative role models, including family, peers, positive rewards (such as money) and instantaneous gratification received from alcohol and other substances must be identified and understood in terms of their effect on the offender's thoughts, beliefs, and behaviors.

Relapse-prevention programs include three phases: assessment of high-risk situations; evaluation of the stage of change the youth is in; and specific assignments designed to enable the youth to develop healthy coping skills. Any circumstance that threatens a youthful offender's self-control increasing his or her risk of relapse, must be identified, understood and alternative strategies for intervention planned. Stages of change that mitigate against relapse include: precontemplation, contemplation, decision making, action, and maintenance. Anyone may take an addictive behavior—smoking, dieting, drinking—and apply these stages to create a relapse-prevention plan. For example, if you were a food addict, precontemplation requires you to think about your experiences and the conditions under which you craved food. You then contemplate having the food, fantasize about how good it tastes, see it, create a way to get it, and then take action. Teaching youthful offenders to recognize these phases and offering them a way to plan to intervene in this cycle enhances their opportunity to resist relapse.

Treatment of Youthful Sex Offenders

In the past, sexual offending among adolescents, including violent juvenile offenders often was ignored or minimized. Such behaviors were dismissed as experimentation. However, research (Abel and Becker, 1993; Schwartz and Cellini, 1995) indicates that over 50 percent of the molestation of young males, and almost 20 percent of female molestation is perpetrated by adolescents. Within their lifetime, adolescent sex offenders may commit nearly 400 sex crimes. This reflects an increase in the sex offender rate of 55 times each year as the offender moves from adolescence to adulthood. Abel and Becker (1993) studied 232 pedophiles and found they had attempted a total of 55,250 molestations of which 38,727 were completed. Each pedophile attempted 238 sexual molestations, and completed 167, on average, victimizing over 17,500 children.

Agee (1996) provides the following definitions to standardize admission and treatment of youthful sexual offenders in juvenile and adult corrections programs:

- **Youthful sex offender**—a person from puberty to legal age of majority, who commits any sexual interactions with a person of any age against the victim's will, without consent, or in an aggressive, exploitive, or threatening manner.

- **Youthful pedophile**—a youthful sex offender engaging in sexual interactions with a significantly younger prepubescent victim, usually at least five or more years younger than the perpetrator.

- **Youthful violent sex offender**—a person under the age of legal majority, who is court committed for one of the following offenses: rape, aggravated rape, sexual abuse, aggravated sexual abuse, rape of a child, sexual abuse of a child, indecency with a child, or incest.

Sex-offender Treatment Programs

Essential to any program for violent youthful offenders, but especially for sexual offenders, is to insure the safety and security for staff as well as offenders. Sexual offenders become targets for abuse and attack from nonsexual abusers within the institution. As such, it is critical to provide a safe environment in which treatment may occur. While it is preferable in most instances to provide sexual offenders separate housing, very often this is not possible. In the absence of a discreet program which provides for separate housing and services for sexual offenders, adult corrections systems must insure that the violent youthful sexual offender is safe from harm by establishing policies and procedures that are clear and concise. In addition, it is imperative to train correctional staff in the areas of adolescent development, sexual-offender program interventions, and appropriate security and supervision interventions, specific to this special needs population. Finally, whether the population is segregated or not, it generally is preferable to single bunk these offenders so as to avoid repeated victimization by more aggressive predators. When this is not possible, consideration must be given to additional staff supervision, especially at night.

Components of Sex-offender Treatment Programs

No matter what technique or modality is chosen for the treatment of sexual offenders, all programs should include the following components:

- **Individualized assessments and treatment plan**. Data should be collected about the violent young sexual offenders to properly identify their needs and classify their risk levels. This information provides a baseline from which treatment intervention may be implemented and progress may be verified.

- **Cognitive behavioral techniques**. These include both *cognitive restructuring* in which young sexual offenders participate in groups to challenge current thoughts, values, beliefs, and attitudes, and replace them with more appropriate ones; and *cognitive skills training,* in which prosocial skills are taught to the offender as alternatives to the antisocial skills they currently use. Together, cognitive restructuring techniques and cognitive skills combine to provide the sexual offenders with a different way of thinking about their world while arming them with more appropriate behavioral skills.

- **Acceptance of responsibility for the committed offense**. The program must include opportunities and activities that allow the offender to accept responsibility for the perpetrated offense. As a result of this intervention, the offender has structured and directed possibilities to explore and understand the sequence of thoughts, feelings, circumstances, actions, and arousal stimuli that caused the sexually aggressive behaviors in the first place.

- **Breaking the offense cycle**. The offender must learn how to intervene into and break the offense patterns of behaviors, before an offense is committed. As insights are acquired, cognitions changed, and skills learned, the offender should have ample opportunity to test the new learning and reinforce the breaks in the offense cycle.

- **Posttreatment support groups**. Posttreatment support groups and continued posttreatment access to treatment must be provided to enable the sex offender to maintain a successful lifestyle. This may be instituted within the institution for long-term offenders, or in the community as the offender is paroled. (See Cumming and Buell, 1996. *Supervision of the Sex Offender*). One goal of sexual-offender treatment programs is **control**, not **cure**. As such, the strategy is much like any other addiction-intervention program.

Empathy Training

One of the goals of cognitive restructuring programs is to have sexual offenders be able to take another person's perspective. Characteristic of sexual offenders is their strong sense of denial, minimization, and self-justification. Sexual offenders, especially adolescents, deny ever participating in offensive sexual behavior. Even if they are caught in the middle of an act, sexual offenders will minimize their actions as nothing out of the ordinary, or everyone does it, or it wasn't any "great shake." In effect, they often justify their criminal sexual activities by stating the other person "wanted it" or "said no, but really meant yes" or "shouldn't have been out there so late at night in the first place." All of these reactions prevent the sexual offenders from identifying with their victims, disallowing them from taking the perspectives of their victims, and inhibiting them from feeling any remorse. In fact, the absence of these feelings empower the sexual offenders to perform criminal actions and exercise control over their victims.

One goal of victim awareness programs is to provide the sexual offender with opportunities to compare and contrast the roles of victim and victimizer, so that the offender may identify those victimizing behaviors that are exhibited in the program and eventually, the community. Another goal is to identify the victims and how they were victimized, thus being able to identify the phases of emotional responses of victims. A third goal is to develop an understanding of and acceptance for the hurtful behaviors toward the victim as well as how offenders also hurt their significant others (such as mother, father, wife, children), and themselves. All of these goals are directed toward the offenders changing their cognitive view of their world and being more open to the impact of their own behaviors on others.

Techniques to teach empathy training and victim awareness include individual therapy, group therapy, and educational approaches to alternative behaviors (skill training). Group therapy is used as a forum to review crimes in detail, and analyze patterns of thinking errors, as well as victim responses. Individual techniques for sexual offenders include keeping "reflection" logs; reading stories and articles about victims and then writing reaction papers; having the offender teach a class on victim awareness, emphasizing the victim's emotional and physical pain; or performing community services. Empathy training is a fundamental core of sexual-offender treatment programs upon which other strategies are based.

Intervention Strategies

Group Counseling. This is a treatment strategy of choice among sexual-offender providers. Sexual offenders are not shy and easily recognize each other's thinking errors, behaviors, and antisocial patterns. Therefore, group therapy is extremely effective with adolescents, especially if the sessions are well structured and facilitated. Group sessions should have a permanent group leader and cofacilitator, preferably one male and one female. The group meeting should be run by offenders within a structured process that includes a brief statement of what is happening and what each offender wants to change. Once offenders provide a detailed review of their own crime, the process of identifying thinking errors, developing an understanding of victimization, developing victim empathy, and initiating relapse-prevention programs, including a plan to interrupt the sexual assault cycle, the counseling is begun. In essence, the group process is designed to facilitate the development of trust among group members. This includes intervening in denial and promoting responsibility for the sexual offenses perpetrated. It also includes participating in cognitive restructuring activities, developing appropriate prosocial skills, practicing relapse-prevention techniques, and interrupting the sexual-assault cycle.

Reflection Logs. These are daily diaries that are a learning tool that helps the offender to begin to practice "self-talk," which is inner verbalizations that help regulate behavior. Reflection logs may be reviewed by the treatment staff or group along with the offender to identify the offender's thinking errors, patterns of minimization of sexual behaviors, and self-justification or denial.

Thinking Errors. This concept was first introduced by Yochelson and Samenow (1976). They posited that criminals think differently from noncriminals, which led to their criminal, antisocial behaviors. Some examples of criminal's thinking errors include:

- Power thrust, which is inflated self-image, pride, and a must-win, me-first attitude
- Inability to empathize, which results from an uncaring attitude, lack of respect for others, and isolation from others
- Victim stance, which results from feeling sorry for oneself, refusing to own one's behavior, avoiding consequences, and feeling unable to meet requests
- Impulsivity, which includes irresponsible decision making, with a here-and-now impatient attitude, and a short-attention span
- Failure to accept obligations and resistance to authority, procrastination, uncooperativeness, and lack of self-discipline
- Poor anger control, which is the inability to recognize triggers that result in anger, one's cues that indicate the onset of aggression, and appropriate means to reduce angry responses
- Faulty problem solving, which is ignoring or denying that a problem exists, and making assumptions that lead to unrealistic planning without any proactive action planning

Anger Management. This intervention is designed to reduce the angry feelings, aggression, and violence that one exhibits. Some of the earlier interventions encouraged individuals to vent their anger by yelling, screaming, and punching pillows, to name but a few behaviors. The thought was to encourage individuals to let their repressed hostility free and not repress these feelings and urges. Travis (1983) reported, however, that people who are most prone to vent their rages get angrier, not less angry. This position is supported by McKay, Rogers, and McKay (1989), who found that "venting anger rarely leads to any real relief or any lasting catharsis . . . it leads, instead, to more anger, tension, and arousal." As such, other technologies, more skill and competency based, were developed. These included interventions by Meichenbaum et al. (1971),

Meichenbaum (1977), Novaco (1975, 1979), Feindler (1979, 1981), and Goldstein and Glick (1987, 1989, 1994).

Analysis of Sexual-assault Cycle. The sexual-assault cycle is a sequence of behavior patterns which trigger and escalate the cognition, emotions, and behaviors that lead to sexual assault. Once offenders no longer deny, minimize, or justify their sexual-assault behavior, then self-exploration may begin. In this process, an analysis of every sexual action is completed so as to identify the antecedents and those cues, both mental and physical, that indicate a sexual-assault cycle is about to begin or escalate. Once this is accomplished, the sexual offender is able to identify those factors that will interrupt the cycle by an array of relaxation, imagery, and action techniques.

Prosocial Skill Acquisition. These are a variety of prosocial skills such as problem solving, identifying feelings, expressing a complaint, identifying the feelings of others, and other skills that offenders who are deficit in social skills are taught. These skills are taught by use of an objective technique that includes modeling, role-playing, giving performance feedback, and transfer training. They allow the offender to acquire those social skills necessary to mitigate antisocial situations, including sexual assaults. These curricula also may include psychosocial-educational subjects such as human sexuality and values clarification. As with substance-abuse treatment interventions, relapse prevention is an important, integral part of the sexual-offender treatment program. Many of the same techniques applied in substance-abuse work are useful here, as well.

Treatment of Neglected, and Sexually and Physically Abused

When we think of violent youthful offenders, we usually envision predators who have committed some heinous acts against people and/or society. Indeed, a majority of the youthful offender population are as we imagine. However, a significant proportion of youthful violent offenders who have committed violent crimes are victims themselves. It is this group to whom we now turn our attention so as to better understand how the general-population offender behavior and culture is augmented as a result of these adolescents.

We already have elaborated in Section One, data that indicate the strong relationship between youthful violent criminal behavior and such social variables as poverty, drugs, lack of education and job opportunities. There is a large body of literature (Ewing, 1990; and Widom, 1992, 1995, 1996) which demonstrates that abused and neglected children are more likely to become violent adolescents and adults. Indeed, Cellini, Schwartz, and Readio (1993) surveyed 105 convicted sex offenders incarcerated in Washington State and found that 47 percent reported that they had committed their first sexual offense before the age of seventeen, but only 7 percent of these were apprehended as juveniles. Of the 75 percent who indicated they had been sexually assaulted, 84 percent said that they later had committed an assault that was similar in nature to their own abuse. Widom (1992), conducted a longitudinal study which examined 1,575 child victims who were identified through court cases. By 1994, almost 50 percent of the victims who were mostly in their late twenties and thirties were arrested for some type of (nontraffic) offense. Eighteen percent had been arrested for a violent crime, and this arrest rate was 25 percent higher among African-American victims.

The behavioral and psychological effects of abuse are well documented. We know the warning signs and observable symptoms associated with abuse and neglect. They include:

- Fear of being approached, touched, or examined by others
- Adolescent prostitution
- Modesty and unwillingness to change clothes or expose any body parts in the presence of others
- Sexual behaviors, references, or vocabulary that are atypical or unusual for the child's age
- Withdrawn or fantasy-filled behavior
- Attempted suicide or talk of suicide
- Extreme changes in school performance and behavior

These signals are critically important for treatment intervention when youth are in their communities. They are also important for the staff who manage violent youthful offenders to know and recognize. These offender types tend to be victims within the prison population and often are abused sexually and physically. As such, they become prey, who others attack. This creates an unsafe environment that leads to other behavior-management problems. By recognizing these offender types and taking preventive steps to safeguard their welfare, the prison staff also prevent further problems within the population. Beyond establishing a safe and secure prison environment, these offenders require many of the same treatment interventions (such as individual counseling, group counseling, and cognitive restructuring), which have been discussed already.

Treating Offenders who are Suicidal

It was 11:05 PM, following shift change, when the correctional officer found offender Jones hanging in his cell. He was only seventeen years old, and no one suspected anything of Jones. True, the last several weeks were difficult because he was recently sentenced to an additional five-year sentence for a new charge from a recent prison incident. He was initially angry, was observed crying and staring at the wall for long periods, and after calling his family, was visibly angry and upset some more. However, he recovered from that, was smiling and seemed in a good mood giving fellow inmates many of his possessions. He was even allowed to stay back during dinner because of a stomachache he had. But he seemed happy after dinner, showed no signs of depression and was seemingly happy.

According to the Centers for Disease Control (1995), the suicide rate among adolescents, especially males, has increased dramatically. In 1950, the community suicide rate for males fifteen to twenty-four years of age was 6.5 per 100,000; and in 1990 it soared to 22 per 100,000. One person kills himself or herself every seventeen minutes. Young men are five times more likely to commit suicide than women; and the rate of suicide among young African-American men is even greater. American Indians and Alaskan Natives have a suicide rate of 64 per 100,000. Among Hispanic males ages fifteen to twenty-four, suicide is the third-leading cause of death. The Centers for Disease Control also reports that 27 percent of high school students think about suicide, that 16.3 percent developed a plan to commit suicide, and 8.3 percent actually made an attempt. Bradley and Rotherman (1989) found that youth who made prior suicide attempts were at the highest risk for future attempts.

We have major problems in our general population. We have an even greater problem in our adult correctional facilities, the very ones in which we now place the youthful violent offender. Nationally, the suicide rate for inmates in detention facilities is nine times greater than in the community (Hayes and Rowan, 1988). In jails and lockups, 19.8 percent of the suicides were among offenders twenty-two years or less. Suicide rates in state correctional facilities are 18 per 100,000. Lyons (1994) found that a large number of prison suicides were among adolescents and that fourteen of New York prison-suicide victims were between the ages of sixteen and nineteen.

Suicide Myths and Reality

Most corrections staff have preconceived ideas about suicide. Consider the following statements, and decide for yourself which are true and based on fact, and which are myths:

1. Suicide usually happens suddenly and without warning.
2. People who make suicidal statements or threaten suicide do not commit suicide.
3. Questioning youthful offenders about suicidal ideation, thoughts, or actions will cause them to kill themselves.
4. People who attempt suicide are still potential suicide risks.
5. Suicide happens more frequently in jails or prison than in the community.
6. You can tell if a person is really suicidal or just manipulating.
7. People who mutilate their bodies are always suicidal.
8. All suicidal persons are out of touch with reality or psychotic.

Now that you have had some opportunity to ponder these, let us take a look at each and determine what is true.

Myth 1: Suicide usually happens suddenly and without warning.

This statement is false. Many successful suicides are carefully planned with thoughtful strategies to cope with serious personal problems. Suicidal persons often give many clues and warnings.

Myth 2: People who make suicidal statements or threaten suicide do not commit suicide.

This statement is also false. Most people who commit suicide have made direct or indirect statements about their intent. If corrections staff listen closely to the youthful violent offenders who are suicidal, they often hear talk about their plans and feeling of self-destruction. Shaffi (1985) found that 85 percent of those suicide victims reviewed expressed their suicide ideation to others.

Myth 3: Questioning youthful offenders about suicidal ideation, thoughts, or actions will cause them to kill themselves.

This is false. Care providers cannot make somcone suicidal, especially if you show interest in their welfare and openly discuss the possibility of suicide. In fact, discussion of suicidal ideation in a nonjudgmental and concerned manner often leads to relief of the youthful offender's psychological pressures and stress.

Myth 4: People who attempt suicide are still potential suicide risks.

Eighty percent of suicide victims made at least one prior attempt. The literature is replete with data that indicate that between 10 and 15 percent of individuals who attempt suicide actually succeed (Schneider, 1954; Maris, 1981; Hirschfield and Davidson, 1988). Neiger (1988) found that of the teenagers who attempt suicide, at least 25 percent have attempted it before.

Myth 5: Suicide happens more frequently in jails or prison than in the community.

This is, sadly, very true. Jail suicides occur nine times more often than in the community; and prison suicides occur at a rate of 18 per 100,000—a third more than in the community (National Center on Institutions and Alternatives, 1995).

Myth 6: You can tell if a person is really suicidal or just manipulating.

We wish we could, but we cannot tell if a person is suicidal. In trying to assess lethality of suicide ideation and threat, perhaps the most critical factor that must be assessed is the offender's *intent* to die. Even if it is determined that the suicide attempt was really a manipulative ploy to control one's environment, the corrections staff still need to involve mental health professionals, insure adequate supervision, and counseling follow up.

Myth 7: **People who mutilate their bodies are always suicidal.**

This is false. Self-mutilation among suicidal offenders is often an act of destruction without the intent to die. Many individuals will self-mutilate because they may have severe personality disorders, may have serious mental disorders, bordering on psychosis, or have extreme attention-seeking needs to be fulfilled.

Myth 8: **All suicidal persons are out of touch with reality or psychotic.**

Most suicidal offenders are very much in touch with reality and in control. In reviewing cases of suicide attempts, gestures, and threats, very few individuals were found to be psychotic, suffering with schizophrenia, or seriously depressed.

Understanding Suicide — One Model

Suicide is a complex human reaction that requires a multilevel approach for understanding. It is simplistic to believe that a violent youthful offender commits suicide as an escape from an emotional state that is hopeless, characterized by despair, rage, or terror. Indeed, to best understand suicide and take actions to mitigate it within the institution, we must explore the population at risk, stressful event factors, the offender's decision (process), and the opportunity to complete the act.

Populations at Greater Risk

According to Brent et al. (1988, 1993) and Shaffer (1994), 90 percent of all adolescent suicide victims have suffered from at least one major psychiatric disorder. Major depression increases the risk of these young people to commit suicide only after the depression begins to lift, since when persons are extremely depressed, they are psychologically and physically unable to attempt suicide. As youthful offenders become less depressed, they feel more energetic, and it is during this period that the offenders are at their highest risk of successfully committing suicide.

Those with a problem of substance abuse are the second major category of the offender population that is at higher risk of suicide. The National Center on Institutions and Alternatives (1988) and Hayes (1988) report that in jails, 60 percent of suicide victims were under the influence of alcohol, drugs, or both at the time of their incarceration. Jacobs (1989) reported that there are between 7,000 and 13,000 alcoholic suicide victims each year. Roy (1989) reported that the suicide rate for heroin addicts is twenty times greater than for the general population. One reason why substance abuse increased the chance of suicide is impaired functioning.

A second reason is withdrawal. Youthful offenders who retreat into their own world, want to be left alone, or complain of illness to feign social interaction should be monitored carefully, since they are at greater potential for suicide gestures and acts.

Another group who should be monitored include those who have attempted suicide previously. As stated before, approximately 80 percent of all individuals who commit suicide have made at least one prior attempt. Family history of suicide is also a strong indicator of suicide risk. A disrupted family environment in which there may be a separation, divorce, death, or family violence also should be noted when dealing with the violent youthful offender. These factors create tremendous strain in a young person's life and often lead to suicide ideation. Finally, Hendrin (1986) and Wolfgang(1958), both found that individuals who have killed others have a suicide rate that is several hundred times greater than those who have not.

Stressful Events

Selye (1956) defines a stressful event as anything that causes an upset or a significant change in the person's life. Typical stressful events may include divorce, loss of a loved one, loss of a job, illness, arrest, or events leading to arrest. We are all aware of the literature that involves suicides among those individuals with terminal diseases. The recent debate with physician-assisted suicides spearheaded by Dr. Jack Kevorkian has raised the national debate on this issue. Schaffer (1988) identified three stressors specifically related to suicide among adolescents: acute disciplinary crisis with fear of consequences; recent disapproval or rejection; and anxiety over an impending change. Callahan (1993) found that confusion over sexual orientation is a newly identified risk factor for adolescents.

Among violent youthful offenders, stressful events which are related to incarceration include:

- Their time of entry. The youthful offender may experience fear, shock, disbelief, and panic.

- Lengthy incarceration. Hopelessness is often associated with extended periods of incarceration.

- Pre- and postsentencing dates. Marcus et al. (1993) found that 40 percent of all suicides occurred within three days prior to or following a court appearance.

- Isolation

- Program and prison transfer

- Denial of appeal/parole hearings

- Disciplinary action

- Another inmate suicide

- Inmate threat or assault
- Dates of personal significance (such as a family member's death)
- Personal loss

The Decision

When violent youthful offenders **decide** to commit suicide, they view the act as an **escape** from unbearable emotional feelings and pain that cause hopelessness. In adolescence, suicide is often an impulsive act, not pre-meditated, and often unplanned (Brown, 1991). Some common interpretations of suicide by young people include: reunion, death as a rebirth, death as retaliatory abandonment, death as revenge, and death as a self-punishment or atonement for one's behavior.

Opportunity

For the violent youthful offender, opportunity translates into unsupervised time to commit suicide. While young people in the community most frequently commit suicide using firearms, followed by hanging, using drugs or by asphyxiating themselves (Garfunkel, 1989), the most common method in a correctional setting is hanging. Death by hanging occurs within three-to-five minutes, and requires only enough pressure to cut off the flow of blood to the brain. Contradictory to common belief, one does not have to jump off the bunk, break one's neck, or be hanging high. Death by hanging is easily accomplished using door knobs, uncovered vents, light fixtures, clothes hooks, and suspended lockers.

What Correctional Staff Need To Do

Identifying suicide risk must be a vigilant ongoing process that starts at reception and continues until a violent youthful offender is released. Staff need to communicate across all lines of function (including security personnel, medical staff, teachers, and program staff) and across shifts. Staff should be mindful and alert for signs of suicide, as discussed previously.

Staff need to be informed. Direct-care staff should know the risk factors for suicide and should know their roles and responsibilities in suicide prevention. Treatment staff and managers in the housing area should be aware of significant stressful events in the lives of the youthful offenders. Officers should know the habits of the inmates under their supervision and be alerted for deviations from those behaviors. All youthful offender communications should be taken seriously, and no one should minimize the statements of youthful offenders. All staff should encourage adolescents to communicate freely and inform staff of suicide talk. Usually, this is a good indicator of what may come. Staff also routinely should observe for suicide-risk indicators and communicate their observation of potential suicide risk to other staff.

Beyond being alert and proactive in their observations, staff must provide appropriate supervision, which is constant according to routine, and irregular spot checks when suicide gestures or behavior is suspected. Staff should be alert to structural or other devices which may be used to attempt suicide. It is critically important to provide timely assessment and treatment when suicide attempts are suspected. Should a suicide attempt be successful, the institution must have a plan which allows staff and youthful offenders time to debrief and process the situation. Other suicide attempts and gestures are at their highest immediately following a suicide.

Special Education Programming

Most adult corrections systems provide some type of educational and/or vocational training to inmates. Usually these programs are under the aegis of General Equivalency Degree programs, Adult Basic Education programs, or some form of tutoring. Unfortunately, with the advent of violent youthful offenders in adult populations, these educational program offerings are sorely inadequate at the very least, not to mention the reality that adult systems may be out of compliance with the State Department of Education's Commissioner's regulations, or even worse, in violation of state or federal law. With the advent of The Education for All Handicapped Children Act (PL 94-142, 1975) as reauthorized by the Individuals with Disabilities Education Act (IDEA, 1990), any individual certified as eligible for Special Education is entitled to a free and public education until that person reaches the age of twenty-one. Even if individuals are incarcerated, legally they have a right to an education, equal and comparable to that provided in public schools.

Indeed, Congress reauthorized IDEA again during their 1997 session and explicitly stated, for the first time, that the act applies to prison inmates who are otherwise eligible. However, prison authorities will not be obligated to screen inmates for special education needs and only will be obligated to provide special education services to those inmates *previously* identified as in need of special education services. While there is no accurate estimate of the number of prisoners who might be affected under the law, a Justice Department survey (1991) found that more than 155,000 state prisoners at that time were twenty-four years of age or younger, and about 10 percent of those inmates had a disability covered under IDEA.

Who are considered special education students? Typically, they fall into categories that include:

- The learning disabled. This is a disability in people who have average or better intelligence and have substantial deficits in one or more academic abilities. For example, a young person with learning disabilities may be highly proficient in math or verbal skills, but be inept in reading or writing skills.

- Mentally retarded. This refers to individuals with significantly low intelligence and adaptive social skills such as dressing, managing finances, or handling functional living skills. These individuals have problems with comprehension, memory, or following directions.
- Seriously emotionally disturbed. This category sometimes is referred to as behavior disordered. In this disability, individuals have severe emotional and/or behavioral problems. Their emotional reactions are extreme and intense. They last much longer than the average for the presenting situations.

Characteristics of Each Disability

Percentage of Youthful Offenders in Each Category

Within the juvenile offender population, approximately 35 percent of adjudicated juvenile offenders have learning disabilities compared to 5 percent of the general population (OJJDP, 1995). The mentally retarded disability represents between 10 and 30 percent of the incarcerated offenders compared to 1 to 3 percent of the general population (Brown and Courtless, 1982). Finally, approximately 35 to 40 percent of youngsters in juvenile settings previously were identified as seriously emotionally disturbed, compared to only 1 percent of the general population (Eggleston, 1984). Of course, many offenders may be in more than one category.

Youthful Violent Offenders with Learning Disabilities

The violent youthful offenders with learning disabilities have problems organizing information; have a difficult time focusing and attending to tasks for more than a few minutes; suffer from short-term memory loss, that is, they have problems remembering things they recently heard or learned; and are easily distracted. Often, caregivers perceive them as confused or haphazard in their behavior. Many cannot follow directions, especially when more than one step is given at a time. Youthful offenders who have this disability are impulsive decision makers, hyperactive, socially naive, and have great difficulty with their peers. They are victimized easily by others and often act aggressively to counteract attacks from others. Often, these offenders appear unmotivated and defiant (beyond typical adolescent behavior).

Youthful Violent Offenders with Mental Retardation

Ninety percent of individuals with mental retardation are "mildly" retarded. In other words, violent youthful offenders with mental retardation often appear "normal," but are a bit "slow." Many of these offenders have difficulty with communication, express themselves with difficulty, and do not provide clear messages about what they are thinking or experiencing. They have difficulty finishing tasks independently and paying attention to assignments beyond a few minutes. These individuals must have simple, concrete strategies, which they may use and learn repetitiously. These offenders are followers and will gain approval from peers by doing favors, acting in bizarre fashions, and being gophers.

Youthful Violent Offenders with Emotional Disturbance

Those juvenile offenders who have serious emotional disturbance either may present themselves as *aggressive* or *introverted*. Aggressive emotionally disturbed offenders externalize their thoughts, feelings, and disturbances. They act out impulsively, and when upset, they become hostile and aggressive. They frequently are rejected by their peers and adults. With little concern for consequences, they participate in power struggles in angry, nonrational ways. Introverted emotionally disturbed offenders frequently appear depressed, anxious, withdrawn, and nonparticipatory. They have feelings of guilt, self-blame, rejection, worry, and fear. Both introverts and aggressive emotionally disturbed individuals have difficulty creating and maintaining relationships. They demonstrate serious learning problems and most would rather not attempt a task rather than fail in trying to succeed. As nonrisk takers, these individuals will resist trying new things and anything they cannot be assured of completing successfully.

Components of Correctional Special Education

Functional assessments provide corrections staff, especially teachers with information on what is required to provide offenders immediate and positive experiences to enhance their learning.

Functional curriculum should be developed, designed, and implemented to meet the specific, individual needs of each offender.

Vocational training should be specifically tailored to meet the needs of the individuals and their specific disability should be identified. Most institutional vocational programs are dedicated to the needs of the system, and, as such, often offenders with disabilities cannot participate in them. Nonetheless, opportunities for job training are critically important for the violent juvenile offenders, who unlike their adult counterparts, will be released while still young and able to work.

Transition services link the violent youthful offender's correctional education program with previous individualized education plans (IEP), which are required by law and regulation, and the educational support services that the individual needs when released. A corollary to this is the concept of wraparound services. This involves coordination and collaboration among all the human service and education agencies within the criminal justice system.

Teacher training and staff development are required to meet the educational and social needs of juvenile offenders who are disabled and in need of special education. Recruiting, training, supervising, and providing support are critical to special educators who provide services to the violent youthful offender.

A competently designed and implemented special education program will allow the adult corrections system to interpret and manage the youthful offender's behavior and meet the required educational and social needs of this population. As such, to the extent that the program is delivered with integrity, behavior management programs and targeted education will vastly enhance the quality of life for the institution's staff and inmate population.

We have attempted to provide the corrections professional with an overview of the special needs of the violent youthful offender who is placed in adult corrections systems. We have concentrated our discussion on those areas which are common among this offender population. As the adult corrections system prepares to accept this new challenge to deal with the violent youthful offender, it must begin to differentiate among programs and services to meet the needs of this population. As such, it is important that all staff have a thorough, working knowledge of the special needs populations within the violent youthful offender class of inmates. We no longer can afford to relegate this information to clinicians, or direct program staff, for the nature of the violent youthful offender population requires that we provide them with a holistic, comprehensive view of their world. Administrators, managers, supervisors, security and program staff alike, will need to be aware of these issues, especially as they impact on the adolescent within our prison systems. We now direct our attention to those areas that involve program design, development, and implementation.

5 Program Design, Development, and Implementation Issues

The Importance of Programs

Those in the juvenile justice system long have known the role and importance that structured, well-organized programs play in the management of juveniles incarcerated in their institutions. Indeed, over the last twenty-five years, much has been researched and written about in this area. We know from section two, that adolescents require deliberate interactive activities, which are well matched to their developmental stages and developmental areas of growth. Toward that end, this section concentrates first on what we know about effective programming, its development, design, and implementation. After we have explored these subject areas, we will devote the remainder of the section to an exploration of the various program models that have been effective with young violent juvenile offenders, whether they are incarcerated in juvenile institutions or in the adult correctional systems.

Nothing Works, Some Things Work, What Works!

Perhaps the most provocative contribution to the program literature involving juveniles was made by Martinson (1974). Some say it was the most deleterious impact on juvenile programs because many policymakers, including politicians, used Martinson's position that "nothing works" to reduce recidivism and alter juvenile delinquency, to reduce operating budgets of juvenile justice agencies throughout the country.

Essentially, Martinson reviewed a broad range of studies reported in the criminal and juvenile justice literature. As a result of that survey, Martinson concluded that most treatment interventions were not effective in reducing criminal behavior or curbing recidivism. It was Palmer (1975) who revisited Martinson's conclusions, and boldly stated that the study was flawed because Martinson failed to consider the specific components of those interventions he reviewed; and, as such, falsely presumed no effect, when, indeed, the detailed analyses of these same studies demonstrated significant statistical and program effects. Unfortunately, even though Martinson (1979) retracted his findings, the impact already affected policy and the antirehabilitation, prodeterrence movement caused a major shift in corrections' practice. These actions impaired offender-treatment programs, sabotaged program budgets, weakened staff attitudes, and undermined citizen support for rehabilitation interventions.

It is clear that some interventions do work. Despite the political popularity of the punishment mode of deterrence, only policies that provide for treatment reduce recidivism. Also, mere punishment is not cost efficient.

There are a number of important contributions made by researchers that support our position that differential and prescriptive treatment does work, especially if the program takes care to answer these questions: (1) what intervention, (2) for which type of clients, (3) meeting with which change agents, and (4) for what outcomes? Answers to these four questions assures that interventions specifically meet the needs of the offender, based upon identified needs.

Meta-Analysis

Meta-analysis is a quantitative approach. It systematically reviews outcome research in which standard measures of magnitude of the effects of the intervention on recidivism are determined for each of the program interventions. Once this is done, an average estimate based on all data available from the studies is conducted. This is followed by some comparative analysis of the aggregate results. Within the correctional systems, several giants in this area have contributed fundamental knowledge to our understanding of what constitutes effective programs.

The Carleton University Meta-Analysis (Andrews, et al. 1990). This group reviewed 154 different pieces of research to determine the magnitude of the relationship between reduced recidivism between an experimental and a comparison condition. Andrews found:

- Official punishment without the introduction of correctional-treatment services does not work.

- What works is the delivery of clinically and psychologically appropriate correctional treatment service, under a variety of settings and conditions that may be established by the criminal sanction.

- Providing correctional treatment services that are not consistent with the principles of risk, need, and responsivity does not work.

- The delivery of appropriate correctional treatment services is dependent upon assessments that are sensitive to risk, need, and responsivity.

The Lipsey Meta-Analysis (1992). This meta-analysis is perhaps the most comprehensive review of corrections treatment literature completed, thus far. Lipsey systematically reviewed those treatment variables associated with reduced recidivism. He concluded that:

- The best treatment interventions were structured and targeted to the population.

- The best treatment interventions reduced recidivism by about 30 percent.

- Methodological conditions influence the size of the effect.
- The best treatments usually were those that had been defined independently as most clinically relevant, as defined by Andrews, Bonta, and Hoge (1990).

Cognitive Behavioral Interventions

One important element we have learned from these various meta-analysis research efforts, is that there are certain types of programs that impact on criminal behavior more effectively than others. As a class of interventions, the cognitive-behavioral programs are those interventions which rely on principles that attempt either to change the offender's thinking process, specifically those attitudes, values, and beliefs which support antisocial, rather than prosocial behavior; or those interventions that teach offenders appropriate prosocial skills to use as alternatives to their skill-deficit repertoire of behaviors.

Research supports the notion that cognitive behavioral programs reduce recidivism. They have an impact on aggressive and violent behavior and can be managed and implemented within the corrections systems, and they easily may be taught to staff at all levels within the system. Beyond that, these programs are accepted readily by the offender population and quickly demonstrate positive change through observable behaviors.

Principles of Effective Programming

There are certain indicators of effective programs. These are based on meta-analysis research, and also on theories of criminal development that include social control theory, strain theory, and social learning theory.

Social control theory asserts that the chief cause of delinquency and criminal behavior is a failure in socialization and bonding to prosocial values and activities. As such, biological, psychodynamic, and psychosocial factors must be considered. Social control theory relies on the notion that it is the social controls within the general society that regulate the frustrated wants and unfulfilled needs of youth.

Strain theory assures that delinquency, and specifically the subcultural criminality found in lower-class adolescents, is a direct result of blocked opportunities to conform. Delinquency, from this perspective, is a response to actual or anticipated failure to fulfill societally induced needs and to meet socially accepted goals and aspirations through conventional channels.

Social learning theory emphasizes the importance of both conventional and deviant social groups, especially peer groups. This theory contends that youth are socialized into delinquency and criminal behavior.

In summary, chronic and serious youthful offenders develop criminal behaviors because of the following:

- Weak controls produced by inadequate socialization, social discrimination and strain

- Strain, which can have a direct effect on criminal behavior and delinquency, independent of weak controls and which also is produced by social disorganization
- Peer group influences that intervene as a social force between a youth with weak bonds and/or strain on the one hand and delinquent behavior on the other

According to Andrews (1994), the clinical principles with the strongest research support are risk, criminogenic need, and responsivity. When we consider risk principles, we must be concerned with our ability to identify lower- and higher-risk cases and insure that treatment services are targeted to higher-risk cases. The major risk factors according to the Carleton Group (Andrews et al., 1990) include:

- Antisocial attitudes, values, beliefs, rationalizations, and affective states such as anger, resentment, defiance, and jealousy
- Antisocial associations that support criminal activity and relative isolation from prosocial peer groups
- A history of antisocial behavior, usually from a very young age, which involves a number and variety of harmful acts in numerous situations
- Weak problem-solving and self-management skills in combination with aggressive, egocentric, noncaring attitudes and behaviors
- Family involvement which is characterized by low levels of affection and little supervision with little or no discipline
- Generalized difficulties in the areas of school, work, recreation and leisure-time activities, with low levels of personal, social, and economic achievements

Curiously, these are not very different than those risk factors first reported by Glueck and Glueck (1950) in their survey of juvenile delinquency and Hirschi (1969) in his survey of self-reported delinquency of school children. Both identified the following risk factors for those juveniles who got in trouble with the law: easily bored, below average in verbal intelligence, weak self-control, violator of many rules, dislike of school, poor family relations, poor parental supervision, antisocial attitudes, and antisocial associates.

Criminogenic needs are those dynamic risk factors (which are represented by intermediate-program targets) which show promise of reducing recidivism. These, in effect, are aimed at the following areas:

- Changing antisocial attitudes
- Changing and managing antisocial feelings
- Reducing antisocial peer associations
- Promoting family affection and communication
- Promoting family supervision and involvement
- Promoting child and family protection

- Promoting identification and association with anticriminal role models
- Increasing self-control, self-management, and problem-solving skills
- Replacing antisocial with prosocial skills
- Reducing or eliminating chemical dependency and substance abuse

As you review the next part of this section, note how the program models described address criminogenic needs.

The concept of responsivity states that treatment programs are delivered in a manner that facilitates the learning of new prosocial skills by the offender. Responsivity matches the treatment approach with the personality and learning style of the juvenile offender; matches the characteristics of the offender with those of the therapist; and matches the skills of the therapist with the type of program available. The concept of responsivity is analogous to the concept of differential and prescriptive programming as described by Goldstein and Glick (1987, 1989, 1994) in much of their work with juvenile offenders and gangs.

Other indicators of effective programming include:

- Setting conditions. This requires that the parameters of the environment, the nature and qualifications of staff, and the nature of offender population to be served be well defined and described.
- Therapeutic integrity. This requires that the program as designed and developed be implemented, without change or modification.

From the several meta-analyses conducted thus far (Andrews et al. 1980 and Mork and Lipsey, 1992), we learn some programs do work and are effective (according to the principles we have outlined). These include social learning strategies, behavioral techniques, cognitive methods, educational interventions, and family-based interventions. Those programs that do not work, or seem less effective include: nondirective, client-centered counseling, unstructured psychodynamic therapies, programs that involve intense group interactions without regard to personal responsibility, and variations on these with punishment and sanctions.

Thus far, we have provided the backdrop for the corrections professional to approach program design, development, and intervention issues. We have attempted to summarize the vast literature available that supports the position that programs do work, and that there are certain interventions that do have an impact on criminal behavior and reduce recidivism. If the corrections practitioner is willing to set the limits and conditions for programs to operate, train staff appropriately in the program principles to implement the chosen intervention, manage and monitor the process, and insure integrity of the program, then optimal results will occur. Given the insights we now have about program design, development, and implementation, we now turn to the variety of program models available to corrections' practitioners in order to manage violent youthful offenders in an adult system. We specifically highlight program models in the domains of education, counseling, health and mental health, recreation, cultural awareness, mentoring, aftercare, and gangs.

Program Models

Education

Education programs and services in adult corrections systems have been limited to either General Education Degree (GED), posthigh school vocational training programs, or posthigh school academic programs such as college and advanced technical school classes. However, with the introduction of the juvenile offender into adult corrections institutions, many of whom are under the age of majority, educational programs and services take on broader program application than before. Specifically, juveniles, especially under the age of sixteen, are required to attend school, and those institutions which house these juveniles must comply with the rules and regulations as promulgated by their state education department. In many states, juveniles who normally would attend high school must attend at least five-and-a-half hours per day of instruction, and those at the elementary level, six.

In 1975, The Education for All Handicapped Children Act (PL 94-142) was passed and was reauthorized as the Individuals with Disabilities Education Act (IDEA) in 1990, and again in 1997. The law guarantees that school-aged youth who have been or are identified as disabled will receive a free and appropriate public education and related services. Many adult corrections systems either are unaware of these statutes or blatantly ignore them. However, until 1997, there was no case law in this area that either directed adult systems to provide these educational services to violent youthful offenders or exempted them from doing so. As we stated previously, with the reauthorization of IDEA in 1997, corrections systems now are obligated to provide special education services to at least a portion of their population. However, it is our contention that there is a broader presumption that all of the violent youthful offenders adjudicated and placed in a corrections facility are considered in need of special education services and fall under these laws. Until the new legislation can be tested in the courts, we need to be cognizant of those principles under which effective educational program models are designed, developed, and implemented. These principles include:

- Free and appropriate public education. Violent youthful offenders should be provided education and related services to meet their education needs free of cost to them or their families.

- Notification and procedural rights for parents. This is vital because the law mandates that parents be notified and give permission before their children are tested or placed in special education.
- Identification and services to all students. The entire youthful offender population must be assessed and services provided.
- Necessary related services. These include those support services such as counseling and remedial services to insure acquisition of learning.
- Individualized assessments. Specific evaluations are needed to assess and then determine the youth's educational levels and needs.
- Individualized Education Program (IEP). This is a written education plan developed by the entire staff involved with the youthful offender, which is reviewed on a regular basis.
- Least-restrictive environment. This should not be confused with the requirement of imprisonment. Rather, this principle requires that the youth should not be isolated from the mainstream of others who are involved in nonspecial education programs.

Correctional education services may be funded through a variety of sources. There are three primary models. One involves the correctional agency being designated as an independent school district and assuming the responsibilities of any local education agency. The advantage of this model is that it allows the agency to receive federal funds directly without having to be a subunit of the state education department. However, unlike the typical local education agency, since there is no constituency which may be taxed, there is no other financial support base, and as such, additional funds must come from the state operations budget. A second model involves the agency being a duly registered education program with the state education department. In this model, the state education program acts as a pass-through agency for federal and state funds. However, the corrections agency, then, must comply with all state education commissioner regulations, which may be restrictive and difficult to implement. The third model is a combination of the two under a special act of the state legislature, which in essence establishes the corrections agency as a "Special School District," and makes it exempt from existing state laws and regulations. The latter is most difficult to enact and implement.

For any correction education program to be successful, Rutherford and Wolford (1987) have identified the following components:

- Functional assessments — of the deficits and learning needs of the offender
- Functional curriculum — targeted to meet the needs of the offender
- Vocational training — in which specific tasks and skills are targeted with the offender

- Transition services — to coordinate the entire offender-education program to the existing corrections agency services
- Comprehensive aftercare education services — either to continue the services provided in the institution; or provide those services when released which insures new skills are applied to a relevant work situation
- Teacher training and support — ongoing staff development activities, which include inservice training, seminars and conferences, and on-the-job training

Counseling

Up until the early 1970s, all counseling interventions were categorized in one of three fundamental approaches:

1. Psychodynamic therapies. These are based on the theories of Sigmund Freud. These approaches require long-term commitment to self-analysis, and rely on strong verbal acuity. In essence, such interventions require individuals to be able to free associate and talk about significant events that will free up their unresolved conflicts as defined by Freud, Jung, Adler, and others. Such interventions may take the form of individual and/or group sessions.

2. Client-centered therapies. These interventions were developed by Carl Rogers and William Glasser, among others. These therapies assume that if the counselor creates an environment that supports unconditional love, mutual respect, and empathy, then the offenders will be able to talk about their feelings and relationships openly and honestly, thus gaining insight into those dynamics that created problems for them in the first place. Again, these interventions require verbal skills, and the ability of the youthful offender to openly discuss their relationship with significant others in order to free up their inner conflicts.

3. Behavior modification therapies. These are those interventions based upon Pavlov, Skinner, and Watson. These interventions use various schedules of reinforcements to modify observable behaviors of the offender. They require consistent and constant monitoring to insure that appropriate targeted behaviors are changed. Such interventions as "level systems," "token economies," "therapeutic communities," "guided group interaction," and "positive peer cultures" are examples of these therapies.

By the 1970s, with the advent of the microchip and the development of the personal computer, statisticians were able to apply the principles of meta-analysis and gave the corrections field new insights into the nature and needs of the juvenile delinquent and youthful offender.

As a result of those analyses, psychology identified a fourth fundamental approach. This was defined as *psycho-social-educational therapies.* These were developed by Bandura, Goldstein, and Glick, among others.

This approach endorses cognitive behavioral interventions that are well researched and found to be effective interventions for young offenders. Among the more popular approaches found to be effective include:

- Aggression Replacement Training (Goldstein and Glick, 1987). This is a multimodal approach to reduce aggression and violence in offenders. The ten-week curriculum consists of social skills training, anger control training, and moral education. Offenders attend a class once each week in each of the three components for one hour.

- Problem Solving Skills (Taymans, 1995). This is an eight- to ten-hour curriculum in which offenders learn the steps to problem solving.

- Cognitive Self-Change (Bush, 1996). This is an eight-lesson curriculum in which offenders are taught to look objectively at their thoughts, values, feelings, and beliefs to proactively and objectively change those thoughts and, in turn, change their behaviors.

- Reasoning and Rehabilitation (Ross and Fabiano, 1986). This is a structured curriculum that attempts to change thinking errors and teach certain social skills. The program requires trainer certification and special training to be implemented.

Health and Mental Health

We already have established elsewhere that adolescence is a period of storm and stress, one of turmoil during which critical tasks are achieved in order to transition into adulthood. A small, but significant number of youthful offenders have mental health issues and are considered mentally ill. Psychopathology refers to behavior that stems from mental disorders. Violent behavior precipitated by psychopathology tends to be intense and fueled by inner emotional dynamics. Since many mental disorders now can be controlled with medicines and/or cognitive-behavioral interventions, it behooves the corrections system to appropriately assess youthful offenders so as to provide the best and most effective interventions, whether they be life-skills training, educational skills, or vocational training.

Little research has been conducted that studies the psychiatric disorders found in youthful offenders committed to adult correctional institutions. There are studies available that demonstrate the prevalence of psychiatric disorders among youth entering juvenile systems, however. Marstellar (1995) studied the prevalence of mental disorders among all youth admitted to youth detention centers in Georgia. A total of 701 youth were evaluated over a month's period of time. Girls were overrepresented in the study. Among the males, Marstellar found the most common disorders were: behavior disorders (36 percent), substance use disorders (30 percent), anxiety disorders (31 percent), and mood disorders (20 percent).

A similar study was conducted in the Ohio Department of Youth Services (Schulz, 1995). He found a prevalence of 18.6 percent for serious mental disorders, which included: schizophrenia, schizo-affective disorders, major depression, bipolar disorder, conduct disorders, and anxiety disorders. Research indicates that most youthful offenders display a blend of many disorders and substance abuse is the most prevalent. Some of the more common disorders found in the youthful offender population include:

- Conduct Disorder — This is the most frequently diagnosed psychiatric disorder in childhood and adolescence. Aggression is the most common behavior.

- Oppositional Defiant Disorder — This is recurrent negative, defiant, disobedient, and hostile behavior of the offender toward authority figures, which lasts at least six months.

- Attention Deficit-Hyperactivity Disorder — This disorder is difficult to diagnose, and commonly is seen in younger children. Usually it is displayed by a short attention span, inability to focus and target behavior, and impulsive behavior.

- Anxiety Disorders — This includes panic attacks, agoraphobia, obsessive-compulsive behaviors, and post-traumatic stress, among others.

- Mood Disorders (Bipolar Disorder, Major Depression) — Symptoms among youth and children manifest themselves differently than in adult populations. In younger offenders, aggression and agitation is often prevalent.

- Schizophrenia — This is rare among young offenders. However, it is not uncommon to find psychotic-type symptoms among young offenders (such as hearing voices, hallucinations and the like); however, they usually are associated with depression and bipolar disorders.

Preferred treatment and program interventions for the mentally disturbed youthful offender includes:

- Peer Communities — Therapeutic communities, positive peer cultures, and guided group interaction are all variations of peer communities and most popular with those with substance-abuse disorders. We use the normal adolescent-development principles of peer influence and environment to provide the most effective treatment intervention.

- Cognitive Behavioral — These therapies have been discussed previously, and they include cognitive restructuring, anger control, and skills-training interventions.

- Victim Awareness — Since many emotionally disturbed and mentally ill youthful offenders do not believe they have done anything wrong, programs in this domain are critically effective in reducing feelings of power and control.

- Drug and Alcohol Counseling — These treatment interventions long have been a part of the juvenile and adult corrections systems. Drug education, Alcoholics Anonymous meetings, and behavior modification techniques are all effective for this population.
- Biological Treatment — Psychotropic medicines to treat psychiatric disorders and control behaviors are effective, only when they are used in conjunction with therapeutic program interventions.
- Psychiatric Hospitalization — This is a last-resort intervention for those psychiatrically disturbed youthful offenders who present a danger and threat to themselves or others.

Health care is another area that is new to those who work with the youthful violent offenders in adult corrections systems. Many of these youthful offenders never have received the basic immunizations against childhood diseases such as measles, chicken pox, whooping cough, and mumps. Some of these youthful offenders have had lifestyles that include drug use, sexual promiscuity, and gang rituals such as tattooing and body piercing. All of these high-risk behaviors have exposed them to a variety of infectious and contagious diseases such as: sexually transmitted diseases (STD's), hepatitis, tuberculosis, and HIV/AIDS. Some of these youthful offenders have been the victims of sexual abuse themselves, which have exposed them to these same risks.

Correctional administrators must work closely with their medical staff to develop a plan which addresses the medical needs of this particular inmate population. The plan should include, but not be limited to, the following areas:

- Review medical policies and procedures to ascertain if any revisions should be made to care for youthful offenders. (Medical personnel should be part of the agency/institutional review team.)
- Review emergency policies and procedures to insure that there are procedures in place in case there is an outbreak of an infectious disease such as measles, chicken pox, mumps, whooping cough, HIV, or tuberculosis. These procedures should include a method to quarantine populations who might be infected and address such areas as visitation and staff safety.
- Provide health education programs developed for youthful offenders. Programs that address the issues of sexually transmitted diseases should be included.
- Provide in-service educational opportunities for medical personnel in adolescent illness, diseases, and injuries.
- Arrange and budget for consultation services of specialists such as pediatricians, and/or physician assistants who specialize in adolescent diseases and injuries. Insure when contracting medical care to an outside vendor, that the youthful offender population is addressed in the contract.

- Develop a budget to immunize all youthful offenders against childhood diseases, if necessary.

Recreation

One of the weakest program areas for juvenile offenders in adult systems is recreation. There are two primary reasons that account for this situation. First, adult institutions traditionally have not concentrated a great deal of effort into this area of programming, spending time and resources in areas of work, training, and education programs. Second, there is little under-standing about the nature of the violent young offender and the specific characteristics peculiar to the adolescent.

Traditionally, adult corrections systems have considered recreation as inmates in the yard for a period of time. In effect, recreation is free time spent in whatever way the inmate chooses when "in the yard." This may be lifting weights (although many adult systems have taken the free weights out of the yards because of safety and security reasons), to playing cards, basketball, or just standing around, "hanging out." The fact is the adults, like their youthful counterparts, lack recreational skills and interests. They are unable to use leisure time constructively. Further, young offend-ers, like adult inmates, have low motivation toward participation in socially acceptable group activities. As such, young offenders are unable to con-structively and prosocially participate in team sports, small group activities, or other recreation activities because they have no will to do so. Finally, even if the violent youthful offenders wish to participate, they have little or no knowledge of what socially acceptable recreation activities are available (Calloway, 1995).

What is the purpose of correctional recreation? At the very least, correc-tional recreational programs relieve the daily tensions that are created by incarceration. These programs attempt to develop leisure skills that person-ally benefit the offenders and carry over into the community, when they are released from prison. Finally, leisure programs can be used as an essential tool for therapy and rehabilitation.

Recreation programs fail to meet their stated goals or purpose for many reasons. First, many programs are poorly designed, and, as such, the de-livery of programs and services often are compromised. Second, sometimes there are inconsistencies between the services necessary and attitudes held by the staff. Third, some recreation programs lead to dehumanizing, degrading, and insensitive methods in their implementation, or actual play. Finally, many programs are poorly managed.

To counteract many of these impediments to successful leisure time, recreation programs for violent youthful offenders, corrections systems should include the following six components:

Leisure Awareness. The recreation staff should identify recreation and leisure-time activities for young offenders.

Self-awareness. A leisure-time assessment survey may be

given to the youthful offenders to identify their areas of interest and competence (Calloway, J. 1996).

Decision Making. Youth need training in skill development to identify alternatives, and to help them make choices.

Leisure Skills. Young offenders should be enabled to develop basic competencies in a variety of recreation activities including: participating in team sports and games; developing skills in particular games such as football, volleyball, basketball, baseball, to name but a few.

Leisure Resources. Staff should develop a list of those areas and people who could provide information and support for leisure time activities.

Social Interaction. By providing social skills and prosocial interaction opportunities, offenders are helped to increase their appropriate mingling and group interaction.

Corrections systems have a variety of leisure time and recreation programs available to them as they serve the young violent offender. These include:

- Arts and crafts
- Clubs, hobbies, and collecting (for example, stamps)
- Dance, drama, and the arts
- Outdoor recreation
- Sports and games
- Music
- Service activities (performing community service, tutoring, and mentoring)
- Social activities
- Mental and linguistic activities (such as *Jeopardy, Wheel of Fortune, Trivial Pursuit*)
- Special events (movies)

We must expand our paradigm, and view recreation programs as a management necessity rather than an institutional afterthought. A well-planned, well-designed, well-implemented recreation service is a useful program and management tool.

Cultural Awareness

Notably absent from most descriptions of effective youthful offender programs, indeed most offender programs, are those issues and attributes that deal with cultural awareness. Yet, practitioners have begun to realize that cultural awareness is critically important to the successful implementation of any program within adult corrections systems. Soriano (1993) defines cultural sensitivity as:

a person's or program's objective understanding, appraisal, appreciation, and knowledge of a particular cultural group that is used equitably in behavioral dispositions towards members of the cultural group. Cultural sensitivity is developed through self-awareness, the elimination of stereotypes and unfounded views, and through gaining objective knowledge and actual interaction with members of a particular cultural group.

Soriano provides us with a paradigm that includes those characteristics that are associated with cultural awareness and sensitivity such as language, ethnic background, cultural training, and staff-capacity building.

It is critically important to apply these concepts to the youthful offender population within adult corrections systems. More specifically, those concepts introduced in Section 2, that identify adolescent stages of development and the physical, cognitive, social, and emotional adolescent domains, now must be applied with Soriano's concepts of cultural sensitivity to implement effective programs and services. Cultural sensitivity to violent youthful offenders requires us to adopt a broader, more sophisticated view of that population. Since these youthful offenders live in various environments that require them to employ multiple social roles, in conjunction with the adolescent social and emotional need to explore their identity, we ought not be surprised that this offender population takes on complex role behaviors. After all, they do function as a son/daughter, brother/sister, employee, friend, member of a cultural group, as well as an offender. Part of their behavior is normal adolescent development and when accounting for the cultural overlay, it becomes critically important that programs attend to these issues as well.

Soriano (1995) suggests multidimensional approaches to ensure cultural sensitivity with violent youthful offenders. He urges a prescriptive approach, which recognizes the multiple identities of the offender group. It is critically important to recognize the developmental stages for those offenders involved in these programs, as well as those staff who need to implement these programs. We suggest, based on Soriano's concepts, that there may be cultural sensitivity in critical tasks that the violent youthful offender must master at each developmental stage. These tasks should include as Pederson (1988) suggests: self-awareness, cultural knowledge, and interpersonal-skill development.

Mentoring

It long has been accepted that role models, heroes, and idols have tremendous impact and exert enormous influence on the thoughts, feelings, and attitudes of adolescents. This is especially true for the violent youthful offender. Indeed, the young offenders often have a profusion of antisocial mentors who guide, support, advocate, promote, and protect them from perceived harm.

Children and adolescents thrive on caring adults who pay attention to them. Normally, young people look toward their parents to provide this function. However, throughout time, other caring adults also have supported them in this role. Historically, before the advent of high technological transportation, when families did not move far from their birthplace, extended families performed the mentoring role well. Grandparents, uncles, aunts, cousins, concerned neighbors, and clergy, all were resources for children and youth. For the violent youthful offender, since their adolescent developmental needs do not change (just because they have committed criminal acts), gangs and antisocial youth groups have replaced the extended family as mentors.

So important is the concept of mentoring, that many community-based youth development programs incorporate mentoring within their services. The Boys and Girls Clubs of America, Big Brothers and Big Sisters, Inc., police athletic leagues, Boys Scouts and Girl Scouts, are examples of a few organizations and youth services that provide mentoring functions to youth. So, too, violent youthful offenders in adult corrections systems require mentors. Programs need to include opportunities for young offenders to be involved with a mentor. Whether a paid staff member or a volunteer, the opportunity for young offenders to be involved with a caring, concerned adult is critically important. There are ample opportunities for this to occur, whether mentoring is provided in school to tutor remedially or for academic deficiencies; or through vocational exploration through various jobs (either paid or not); or for learning nontraditional skills (arts, crafts, ceramics) during which time adult-youth relationships are built.

A variety of organizations are willing to collaborate with corrections systems to provide mentoring services. Church groups, service organizations (such as the Masons, the Lions, the local Rotary), colleges and universities, and private not-for-profit organizations (such as Mentoring USA) are all resources for corrections systems that might serve the violent youthful offender. Each of these organizations provides opportunities that will enhance the thinking, values, beliefs, and attitudes of the youthful offender in a prosocial manner.

Aftercare

Aftercare services are underused within adult corrections systems. Offenders are sentenced to a period of time in prison. If the offenders meet standards of the prison system, they become eligible for parole, and may be released before their entire sentence is served. However, if they do not follow the conditions of their parole, they may be returned to prison to complete the rest of their sentence. Offenders also may opt to complete their entire sentence, that is "bottom out" in prison, and then they are not obligated to serve any time on parole.

Aftercare services is a much different concept than parole. Aftercare is used extensively in juvenile justice systems and is planned as part of the juvenile's placement in the system. It is based on the fundamental premise that the programs and services, which are provided to the juvenile offenders while institutionalized, must be continued for a period of time after the juveniles' release back in their own communities, to insure their continued growth and development, acquisition of skills and competencies, and to reduce recidivism. Aftercare services planning begins at the point of adjudication and placement in the system, and continues during every phase of placement, involving all those staff with whom the juvenile interacts.

Altschuler and Armstrong (1991, 1995) have designed and implemented the Intensive Aftercare Program (IAP). The goals and the underlying principles of the Intensive Aftercare Program program include:

- Preparing youth for progressively increased responsibility and freedom in the community
- Facilitating the youth's interaction and involvement in the community
- Working with both the offender and targeted community support systems (such as families, peers, schools, employers, recreation agencies, and social service agencies)
- Developing new resources and supports when needed
- Monitoring and testing the youth and the community on their ability to deal productively with each other

Program elements for a sound, effective, and efficient aftercare program should first include organizational and structural characteristics in which the size of the system, the philosophical foundations and ideology of the system, the public and private stakeholders, and the number and type of aftercare programs offered should be considered and coordinated. Case management is yet another element of an effective aftercare program. According to Altschuler and Armstrong (1995), case management is the overarching mechanism necessary to achieve continuous, consistent, and coordinated program planning in the Intensive Aftercare Program. Case management traditionally has included the following elements:

- Developing assessment, classification, and selection criteria
- Individual case planning
- Integrating surveillance and services based on risk factors
- Balancing incentives and graduating sanctions
- Providing service brokerage with community resources and linkage to social networks

The third element of an effective aftercare program is the management of information and program evaluation. This component often is overlooked or ignored by program planners and implementers. Yet, it is critically important to substantiate program effectiveness, provide a database to make critical policy decisions and program modifications, as well as defend and justify the program to stakeholders, especially those who financially and politically support (or oppose) the program.

Gangs

Dealing with prison gangs and gang activities has become an integral part of today's correctional environment. Many state and county correctional systems have created gang intelligence units to identify gang members placed in their facilities, coordinate and manage gang activity, and gather gang intelligence within the institution. With the introduction of youthful offenders into adult facilities, correctional administrators need to assess how this new inmate population affects the current gang identification and management procedures and techniques.

During the late 1970s, up through the 1980s and 1990s, we learned a great deal about both prison and street gangs, how they operate within correctional facilities, and on the street. This knowledge, although very helpful in getting an idea on gang dynamics and activities, also can cause a false sense of knowing all there is to know about gangs and what gangs do. Sometimes, maintaining a closed-gang paradigm permits the gangs we are supposed to be observing to change their operations and activities without our even realizing it has occurred. The following examples illustrate this very important observation:

- In the 1980s, community gang intelligence, for months, were unable to identify new gang spin-offs, which already were known to prison officials. This was because all those concerned with gangs and gang activities were complacent that they knew all there was to know about gangs.

- Once some of the gangs found out that certain markings (tattoos, branding, hair styles) or gestures (hand signs) were methods used to identify them, they stopped using these signs and signals. Some correctional and law enforcement personnel felt, that because they no longer observed these outward manifestations, their gang problems were diminishing or at least stablilized. Little did they know, at the time, that new and/or spin-off gangs were forming and were more virulent.

We need to be critically clear about the differences between the adult prison gang and the youth street gang. The youth street gang, oftentimes, is a loosely organized group of adolescents, undisciplined, and impulsively violent. Adult prison gangs are structured, well managed, and very directive in their rules and operations. Juvenile street gangs use violence where adult prison gangs use violence, as a last resort. As such, these differences create friction between the two entities within the prison, partly due to their structure, and partly due to the nature of the adolescent. Other variables include: age, the youth bonding with each other for self-protection and identity, and housing assignments, since juveniles often are separated, as required by local statute or federal regulation.

Of critical importance is what happens to youthful offenders who are placed in adult systems, once they become aware of the prison rules and what is required for their survival. In actuality, violent youthful offenders are perceived as leaders, not because of their leadership abilities, but because they are the most violent. They, like the schoolyard bully, will beat up another inmate impulsively. In reality, with time, the relationships the youthful offenders have with the street gang withers, especially if there is no reason or support for holding fast to their street gang affiliations. This change in relationships and affiliation should not be construed as the violent youthful offenders changing their beliefs, values, and attitudes toward gangs or their gang habits and behaviors. Rather, these young offenders merely are realigning their roles and relationships in order to survive in their new environment.

Taylor (1990) defines three stages of street gang development: scavenger, territorial, and organized/corporate. The scavenger gang is characterized by members who often have no common bond beyond their impulsive behavior and their need to belong. Scavenger gang leadership changes daily or weekly. They have no common goals and no purpose to their organization. Scavenger gang members generally are identified as low achievers and illiterates with short attention spans. They are prone to violent, erratic, behavior. The territorial gangs designate something, some-place, or someone as belonging exclusively to the gang "turf." When scavengers become serious about organizing for a specific purpose, they enter the territorial stage. During this stage, gangs begin to define themselves and someone assumes a leadership role. It is the process of shaping, forming, and organizing with specific objectives and goals. Once the gang has defined its territory, the next step is to defend that territory from outsiders. Gangs defend their territories to protect their particular business. The organized/corporate gangs are well-organized groups which have very strong leadership and managers. The main focus of this organization is participation in illegal money-making ventures. Discipline is comparable to that of the military, swift and severe. Unlike the scavenger gangs, crimes are committed for a purpose, not for fun.

Understanding Taylor's stages of gang development will assist correctional personnel to observe and identify at what stage youthful offenders are, and the sophistication of gangs which may be present. As an example, many youthful offenders in adult institutions band together for protection from older inmates. A correctional caseworker provided the following testimony: "Youthful offenders are homophobic to a point of being ridiculous. They are terribly afraid of being raped by the adult inmates." As such, they band together for protection.

In our work with adult corrections systems which must deal with youthful offenders, we have found yet another phenomenon which we identify as the hybrid gang. The hybrid gang leader (and member) has synthesized those skills and critical tasks integrated from both the knowledge and experience of the street gang and the prison gang. They also have been able to survive and learn the rules of the street and the prison necessary to provide direction and protection to others within the institution.

If permitted to develop from the scavenger stage into the more advanced stages of gang organizations (in other words, territorial and then corporate), these youthful offender gang leaders and their gang members will develop their skills and knowledge in leadership and organization from the two environments to which they have been exposed and in which they have been forced to survive (the streets and the prisons) and the get-tough policy that places youthful offenders in adult facilities. The combination of these environments potentially creates an unanticipated by-product: hybrid gangs with gang members who are very sophisticated and knowledgeable.

They will be sophisticated because they have first hand experience with the authorities of the criminal justice system. They have learned about the adult corrections system at an early age, and have discovered its weaknesses, flaws, and shortcomings. They may have developed methods of taking advantage of it. Taking advantage of the system is not something new for gangs; they have been doing it for at least the past twenty years. Gang members have had courts subpoena them so that they could come together to discuss gang business; they have joined chapel choir groups to review potential candidates for membership, and they have volunteered to work at menial jobs so that they are able to communicate with one another, to name but a few examples of their manipulations. One would be foolish to think that the youthful offenders would fail to develop their own methods of manipulating the system for their own purposes. This is why correctional administrators today will have to make it part of their jobs to understand the stages of gang development and be able to respond to the ever-changing dynamics that gangs present in correctional facilities.

The system already may have started to create these hybrid gang leaders and members by incarcerating youthful offenders in adult facilities, which gives them additional status and prestige with their street associates. Some department of youth services' workers observed that there are juvenile offenders coercing their attorneys to have them bound over to the adult court so that they can do some adult time because that is viewed by their peers as "being cool;" and that, in adult facilities, they "don't have to do nothing," referring to the idea that when incarcerated in juvenile facilities they have to participate in programs.

The gangs, whether youthful offender or adult, have the ability to change their appearance rapidly, have acquired methods to communicate and conduct business efficiently, and have established requirements for membership and/or leadership. However, the system, because of its bureaucracy and often closed paradigms, is slow to recognize and adjust to these changes.

Prison systems should start to refine their strategies to manage youthful offenders' gang development in adult correctional facilities. Some suggestions for these proactive strategies include:

- Instruct staff in Taylor's stages of gang development. (Taylor, 1990)
- Develop a gang intelligence web chart (Sturgeon, 1995). (See Chart 5.1 on page 123)

One mistake is to assume that current gang management techniques will continue to work with these incarcerated youthful offenders. As correctional facilities embark on developing new strategies, they should include defining and identifying the power, profit, and control of gang dynamics (Sturgeon, 1993):

Power. This is needed to make things happen within the institution. This includes knowing things that are supposed to be known only by staff (such as upcoming shakedowns or changes in the daily schedule). Youthful offender gangs sometimes use indiscriminate means to reinforce this perception of power and violence.

Profit. This is any gain in material things that can be spent or bartered. Profit could be money, but it also could be postage stamps, canteen, or other goods and services which are valuable to the offender population.

Control. This is the pretense of having more influence over events, assignments, safety, and security, than they really have. Adult gangs, for the most part, use violence to maintain their pretense of control over profit centers that they control.

Youthful offender gangs overtly have to exhibit their pretense of power and control to the inmates and staff. They have to let everyone know who they are and what they are about. They do this by appearing to take over areas such as: recreation yards, dayrooms, use of the telephones, and living areas. The staff should pay special attention to any area where it appears that the staff have to demonstrate their authority (power) and take control of the area. Staff may exhibit their authority and regain control by the following:

- Staff always must do their jobs and never abdicate their responsibilities.
- Staff should reduce the number of gang members in a given area at a given time.
- Staff should use the disciplinary system to mete out sanctions that meet the offense in a timely manner.
- If the agency has a "zero gangs tolerance" policy, insure that it is well thought out and comprehensive, and that it is consistently enforced.

Remember, wherever there is a (real or imaginary) power/control void, the gangs will move to fill it, and in doing so, will perpetuate the perception that the gang is more powerful and in more control than the administration.

CHART 5.1

INTELLIGENCE WEB FORMAT

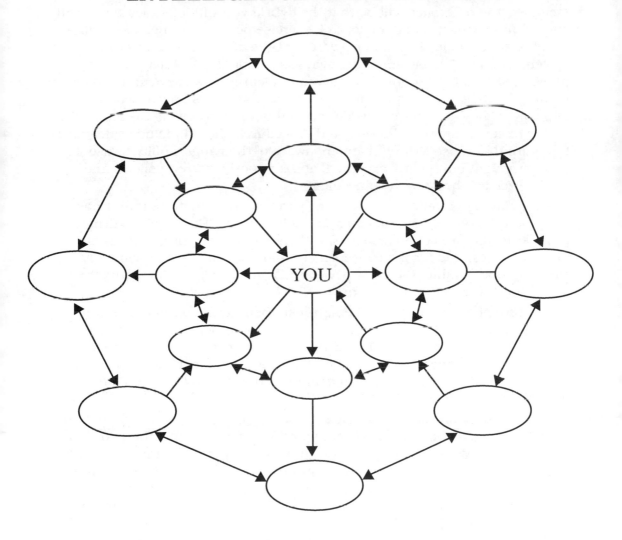

ASSIMILATE
ANALYZE
VALIDATE
PRIORITIZE
DISSEMINATE

We believe that incarcerating youthful offenders in adult facilities will create a type of hybrid inmate/gang member. These hybrid "youthful offender" gangs will clash with the already-established prison gangs for the power/control/profit of the same areas in the facilities where a void in power/control exists. This happens now between rival prison gangs in the facilities. The difference will be that the hybrid youthful offender gangs will employ more violence to gain control, exercise power, and increase their profit. Also, agencies have to be aware that the official activities of the system (such as job assignments, living assignments, and disciplinary process) should be thoroughly analyzed to identify how they can be manipulated by the gangs to give the appearance that gangs have the power and control of what goes on inside the facility, thereby giving the gangs the ability to generate profit. Policies and procedures should include safeguards to insure that those writing them are aware of the gangs' ability to use poorly thought out, poorly executed, and/or poorly written policies and procedures for their own advancement.

After gaining power and control, the gang can demonstrate that it has the power to control both official and unofficial activities, such as drug trafficking and protection schemes. It then can derive a profit by charging for its services, and for the conveniences and necessities of prison life. Also, the gang that exhibits the most power and control will use its status to attract and recruit new members.

Youthful offender gang members, unlike their adult counterparts, will be more apt to use impulsive violence to maintain their power and control, not taking into account how this could affect their profits. By contrast, adult gangs use violence very deliberately, and then for the most part, only when it is absolutely necessary to maintain control and/or intimidate the prison community.

The traditional mechanisms used to control the adult prison population do not seem to work with the violent youthful offender population, and in particular, gangs. There are, however, proactive methods agencies can take to control gang activity within an institution. If adult corrections administrators simply accept that formal gangs and gang activities are routine situations when operating an institution, then those charged with maintaining law and order within the system have relinquished the power and control over the operations of the facility. Such excuses as there is insufficient staff to control what goes on, or to have a gang intelligence unit, are just that—excuses. Administrators must adjust their paradigm and attack the gang problem in prisons using those strategies that they know work. They must continue to look for and try new interventions. Remember that gangs are dynamic, not stagnant. As such, our methods to deal with gangs should be dynamic, not stagnant. Below are some suggestions for proactive strategies to deal with gangs:

- Identify what gangs, both street and prison, currently exist in the facilities. Too often, all of an agency's time and energies are devoted to identify those gangs that are incarcerated. Although it is important to identifying gangs within a facility, it is only the beginning of how an agency will manage gangs and gang activities. The gang-identification process should not stop at the reception and diagnostic facility; it must be implemented throughout the system. Correctional staff should be instructed in ways to identify gangs, gang members, inmates who have joined a gang while incarcerated, new gangs formed within the facility and/or splinter groups/gangs, and know how to report this information.

- Know what gangs, street and/or prison, are currently in power; detail the power priority ladder of the gangs that are in the facility. This power priority ladder should list the most powerful gang on the ladder and then, in descending order, list the remaining gangs. The power-priority ladder should indicate the leaders of the respective gangs, the other officers of the gangs, and all the members. Continuous input from line staff is critical to the success of this strategy because these positions of power and leadership are situational and may vary according to how much power, control, and profit is available.

- Know what the current recruitment requirements are for gang membership. Corrections systems should know the recruitment requirements for membership into the gangs. Requirements could range from belonging to a certain race or living in a certain geographic area. Knowing these requirements will help to identify potential gang members and identify changes in recruitment requirements so that the gang can have more members, thus expanding its power and control.

- Current initiation requirements/rituals for gang membership are important areas for agencies to know. Prior knowledge of requirements/rituals may assist staff in controlling gang activities. Very often, these events are concentrated around violent acts either on the person(s) being initiated or on rival gang members and/or the introduction of contraband into the facility—usually drugs or weapons. Identify areas where the gangs could gain an appearance of control and power and/or where they may have their profit centers. Perhaps this is the most important part of gang management. Identifying and then eliminating areas where the gangs derive their power and control, thereby, eliminating the gang's profit centers, is a proactive way of handling gang management.

A gang's plan is similar to a business scenario where a company has a business plan and in the business plan the rival companies' market share, market domination, and profit centers are detailed for takeover and/or elimination. When identifying the areas where gangs could be working to gain power and control, it is important to be very specific and remember to keep an open paradigm. Remain constantly vigilant for changes in gang activities. Specifically, one should:

- Detail strategies, and create an action plan to eliminate the possibilities of gangs taking over an area. This plan should be detailed and should include goals and milestones.

- Develop a zero gang tolerance policy and articulate it in writing (what it really means and how it will be administered).

Too often, agencies initiate zero gang tolerance policies without thoroughly thinking through what should be included. The following is an example of a detailed zero gang tolerance policy, along with those areas that should be considered by any agency considering a zero gang tolerance policy:

1. Is there an operational process in place to deal with youthful offenders who want to get out of a gang? This includes consideration of the following areas:
   - Housing
   - Removal of tattoos
   - Transfers
   - Educational opportunities
   - Notification of family members

2. Does the policy extend to visitors?
   - Clothing
   - Display of tattoos
   - Display of hand signals

3. Does the policy include written materials from outside of the prison?
   - Newsletter type written materials
   - Articles in newspapers regarding gang activities; can they be displayed or even kept by inmates?

4. Does the visiting policy address the agency's zero gang tolerance policy?

5. Do not try to announce a zero gang tolerance policy unless it can be implemented continuously. To try to implement a zero gang tolerance policy and fail only acts to reinforce the perception that the gangs are in control and will prevail.

All departments within a system can add their own strategies to this list to deal with youthful offenders, gang development and activities as well as indicate what should be included in a zero gang tolerance policy. Corrections systems have the opportunity to interrupt the cycle of gang formation by training the staff in Taylor's stages of gang development and by developing a strategy for those individuals who either want out of gang activity or who do not want to get involved with gang activity, in the first instance.

We have attempted in this section to provide the reader with the principles by which effective programs are designed, developed, and implemented. We have reviewed the major and fundamental program areas, which must be addressed by any adult corrections systems that must serve the violent youthful offender. It is incumbent upon policymakers, administrators, managers, supervisors, and line staff to understand the principles inherent in effective and efficient programs. Within the context of expanded, newly broadened paradigms, the adult corrections systems must be prepared to reinvent their services to better manage this newest offender population. In our closing section, we challenge the adult corrections system to seize the opportunity and continue to serve the public's best interests.

6 Current Practices and Resources

We have just begun this journey of managing violent youthful offenders in adult corrections systems. "Yes, this may be a fine mess that we have gotten ourselves into," as Hardy states. However, given the knowledge and state of art, the quality and caliber of people within our systems, and a change in our paradigms, we have a good chance to be successful in turning around some young lives.

We are optimistic and hopeful that while we deal with only the most violent youthful offender, representing but one-half of 1 percent of the entire youth population, our efforts may extend far beyond our initial interventions. If we believe that each one of these young people potentially represent a generation, then these too are our most precious investment, and they must be nurtured.

If on the other hand, we believe, quite pessimistically, that each one of these youthful offenders represents a horrible plague upon our communities and society, who must be put away and punished, then it might be better that we save our scarce resources and eliminate them at the very outset. Harsh as it sounds, if by our actions, we write off these young people as dregs and an albatross about society's neck, then why not expediently solve the problem, cost effectively. We are quite facetious in this regard, and we do not endorse this position nor believe it to be true. That is why it is so critically important that the message of hope, habilitation, and what works, is essential to broadcast throughout our corrections systems, communities, and among our families and friends.

Toward that end, we now turn to those current practices and resources that are available to the profession as it undertakes the task of managing the violent youthful offender in adult corrections systems. Resources, for the practicing professional, must be those materials, ideas, sources of information, technical assistance, financial support, community advocates, systems, organizations, and networks that assist the practitioner to be successful in a safe and secure environment. There are a variety of arenas in which this may be accomplished. We identify three.

Professional Organizations

When groups of individuals coalesce with a common philosophy, mission, goals, objectives, needs, and training, they often form an association or society to help meet those goals and find common ground to accomplish their mission. So too, corrections professionals have a variety of resources available to them to help provide support, assistance, training, advocacy, and a common core from which new ideas flourish.

The American Correctional Association (ACA) is the oldest professional association for corrections workers. It has become the benchmark for corrections standards and professional practice. Through its various chapters and affiliates, ACA provides conferences, seminars, products, books, journals, research, and member services (such as discounts for purchases, insurance plans, and other benefits) to all those who voluntarily join. The ACA Annual Congress has become a mecca for professional development, networking, product and materials dissemination, social events, and the source of seminal policy development. The professional development division of ACA recently has developed some material on youthful offenders in adult facilities, and a sequel to this work that provides a closer look at many of the considerations raised here is in the works.

Governmental Agencies

The National Institute of Corrections (NIC) was born out of the Attica Prison Riot of 1972. As a result of its investigations, the federal government realized that corrections practitioners required a great deal more training than they had previously received in areas of population management, program design and implementation, offender classification, safety, and security. The National Institute of Corrections was created to provide training and technical assistance to the corrections field.

More recently, as the public policy to incarcerate youthful offenders in adult institutions becomes more prevalent, the need to provide information and training to those who work in these systems with this population became more apparent. The National Institute of Corrections has developed a strategic plan along two parallel tracks. First, it set out to identify effective interventions with high-risk offenders, responding to Martinson's original admonition that nothing works. As such, it had garnered the best minds throughout North America to identify those programs that do work, using much of the philosophy and research of Andrews, Bonta, and Gendreau.

Second, the National Institute of Corrections initiated the development of a curriculum that would assist agency/institutional staff to design and develop effective systems to manage violent young offenders in a constitutionally defensible, humane, adult correctional environment. As a result of that effort, a twenty-seven module curriculum was designed and currently is being offered to jurisdictions through small technical assistance grants. The curriculum is skill based, practitioner-oriented, relevant, and flexible. It allows the receiving agency the opportunity to design its own thirty-six-hour training program based on its own need.

The Office of Juvenile Justice and Delinquency Prevention (OJJDP) was established in 1974 as part of the Juvenile Justice and Delinquency

Prevention Act. Its mission is "to provide national leadership in addressing the issues of juvenile delinquency and improving juvenile justice." As a result of that mandate, the Office of Juvenile Justice and Delinquency Prevention provides leadership, sponsors research and training initiatives to improve the juvenile justice system, and provides direction, resources, and technical assistance to the juvenile justice community.

An offshoot of the Office of Juvenile Justice and Delinquency Prevention is the **Coordinating Council on Juvenile Justice and Delinquency Prevention**, which was established as a separate, independent organization under Section 206 of the Juvenile Justice and Delinquency Prevention Act, as amended. The function of this agency is to coordinate all federal programs that address juvenile delinquency, detention, or care of unaccompanied juveniles, and missing and exploited children.

Clearly, the support services and direction for juvenile corrections is well articulated among these three agencies. In areas of policy formulation, technical assistance, and financial support, the efforts of the corrections practitioner who serve the youthful violent offender can be enhanced.

Foundations

Foundations are yet another resource for adult corrections systems that serve the youthful violent offender. These private, not-for-profit organizations usually have annual goals or special projects they wish to fund. Most use either a mechanism such as a Request for Proposal (RFP) which asks for agencies to submit their ideas for which funds will be provided based upon successful review and competition. The RFP usually specifies the parameters of the service requested and leaves it to the applicant to create the design and implementation. A dollar cap usually is specified so that the funds are managed by the foundation rather than driven by the applicant's proposal.

A second mechanism often used by foundations is the Notice of Fund Availability (NOFA). This approach has a specific model which is expected to be implemented along with a specified amount of money allocated for the program and/or service. The foundations, in this case, seek to have agencies apply to provide the service; and the Notice of Fund Availability specifies the qualifications and requirements in order for the agency to apply for the available funds.

While there are many foundations which provide funds to the criminal and juvenile justice systems, there are a few which consistently and generously give to youth programs and services. Some of these include the following:

- **The Annie E. Casey Foundation**, 701 St. Paul St., Baltimore, MD 21202, (410) 547-6600

- **The Bristol-Myers Squibb Foundation**, 345 Park Ave., New York, NY 10154, (212) 546-4000.

- **The Reader's Digest Foundation**, 2 Park Ave., New York, NY 10016, (212) 251-9800
- **The Ford Foundation**, 340 E. 43rd St., New York, NY 10017, (212) 573-5000
- **The W. K. Kellogg Foundation**, 1 Michigan Ave. E., Battle Creek, MI 49017, (616) 968-1611
- **The Edna McConnell Clark Foundation**, 250 Park Ave., New York, NY 10177, (212) 551-9100

Future Directions

As we continue on this journey toward serving the violent youthful offender in adult corrections systems, we are at a crossroads and must choose which way to continue. Without changing our existing paradigm and pushing our paradigm window to its limit, we easily will continue what traditionally has been done, with little or no meaningful change in the lives of these young offenders. However, if we consider boldly what potentially can be accomplished with this offender population, we will be able to make vast contributions to the art and science of our profession.

Consider for a moment the following:

- Adult corrections systems are faced with both a challenge and an opportunity. The challenge is having to accept the public policy to place violent youthful offenders in adult corrections institutions and programs. The opportunity is to expand the existing paradigm for these youth from only controlling the population to providing experiences that foster individual offender growth and development.

- The traditional laws, regulations, and policies are not applicable for the violent youthful offender. As such, the adult corrections system has a chance to reinvent their organizations to make them more effective and efficient for all offenders.

- Current statutes may not be applicable to efficiently operate the corrections systems, thereby providing opportunities to system administrators to reeducate the legislators, community, citizens, and other stakeholders.

- Issues of restorative justice, which insures that victims of crimes are integrated into the rehabilitation process, are philosophically related to the issues of adolescent development. Adolescent development is concerned with teaching responsibility and prosocial interactions, two goals shared by restorative justice programs.

- Violent youthful offenders have committed some heinous acts, indeed. However, they are still in an extraordinary period of growth and development, which allows the corrections systems to provide opportunities for tremendous learning. As detailed in Section Two, these youthful offenders are ripe to internalize skill development in the cognitive, emotional, and physical domains of adolescent development.

- There is potential for staff who want to be involved with this population to develop new, portable skills and competencies, which will advance their own professional growth and development.

Yet, the adult corrections system is on the precipice of disaster. The violent youthful offender presents some tremendous burdens to the system. Their housing, special program needs, individualized attention, impulsivity, erratic behavior, and unpredictable situational reactions certainly compromise security. However, more critically, each represent potential hazards to the orderly operation of the entire system. Within that vast structure, external stakeholders, both opponents and proponents of this new public policy to place youthful offenders into adult systems, will scrutinize every action, every incident, and every maneuver that is taken.

Careful management of all these issues, along with a coordinated staff involvement, provide an infrastructure to ameliorate many of these issues. However, rather than providing strategies for specific situations, we encourage individuals and organizations to assess their own systems to: identify its strengths and weaknesses when serving the violent youthful offender; identify difficult issues which need administrative attention; recommend those areas that need to be redesigned, developed, or eliminated; and reassess their own capacity to deal with the youthful offender population.

When looking at where we have been, and where we need to be, we must consider carefully what we are doing because what we have designed previously probably is not effective for either the current or the future situation. If we do not take the time and care to develop appropriate, adolescent-relevant programs and services, then we certainly will provide this youthful offender population an environment with which to fill their vast reservoirs with what currently happens in prison. That will allow these young felons to use their own resources and develop into a more vicious hybrid of street youth and experienced inmate. Knowing that most of these young people will not spend more than three-to-five years in prison, on average, we will have created an even greater risk to the safety and social order of our communities.

Our epilog does not end with pessimism, however. Rather, we entrust that our information has provided the field with a knowledge base to dream positive solutions to a most difficult problem. We believe that a vast majority of corrections staff are good, conscientious people who want to make a difference. Certainly, none of corrections personnel expect to become wealthy as a result of their work. Many are committed to contribute to the good and welfare of their society, and yearn for knowledge and strategies to accomplish that commitment. Indeed, there are jurisdictions that already have taken up the gauntlet and have begun to address the issues posed by this new offender within the adult corrections systems. There are laboratories to be accessed, which will provide the field with the resources to develop tactical next steps which may resolve this critically important policy issue. We look forward to studying and reporting on those efforts.

References

Able, G. G., and J. V. Becker. 1993. An Integrated Treatment Program for Rapists. In R. Rada (Ed). *Clinical Aspects of the Rapist.* New York, New York: Grine & Stratton.

Able, G. G., J. V. Becker, W. D. Murphy, and B. Flanagan. 1981. Identifying Dangerous Child Molesters. In R. Stuart (Ed.) *Violent Behaviors: Social Learning Approaches to Prediction, Management and Treatment.* New York, New York: Brunner/Mazel.

Agee, V. M. 1996. Treatment of Youthful Sex Offenders in Adult Institutions. In *Managing Violent Youthful Offenders in Adult Corrections Systems.* Longmont, Colorado: National Institute of Corrections.

Altschuler, D. M., and T. L. Armstrong. 1991. Intensive Aftercare for the High Risk Juvenile Parolee. In T. L. Armstrong (Ed.) *Intensive Interventions with High Risk Youths.* Monsey, New York: Willow Tree Press, Inc.

———. 1995. Managing Aftercare Services for Delinquents. In B. Glick and A. P. Goldstein (Eds.) *Managing Delinquency Programs That Work.* Lanham, Maryland: American Correctional Association.

American Correctional Association. *Corrections Today.* July 1997. Lanham, Maryland: American Correctional Association.

American Medical Association. 1982. Resolution on Television and Media Violence. Annual Meeting. Washington, D.C.

American Psychiatric Association. 1987. Testimony Before Congressional Joint Committee on Television and Media Violence. Washington, D.C.

American Psychological Association. 1994a. *Reason to Hope.* Report of the Commission on Youth Violence. Washington, D.C.

———. 1994b. Task Force on Television and Media Violence. Washington, D.C.

Andrews, D., J. Bonta, and R. Hoge. 1990. Classification for Effective Rehabilitation: Rediscovering Psychology. *Criminal Justice and Behavior.* 17, 19-52.

Andrews, D. and J. Bonta. 1994. *The Psychology of Criminal Conduct.* Cincinnati, Ohio: Anderson Press.

Andrews, D. and J. J. Kiessling. 1980. Program Structure and Effective Correctional Practices: a Summary of the Cavic Research. In R. R. Ross and P. Gendreau (Eds.) *Effective Correctional Treatment.* Toronto, Canada: Butterworths. Pp. 441-463.

Barker, Joel A. 1990. *The Business of Paradigms.* Austin, Texas: Barker Associates.

———. 1993. *Changing Paradigms*, Videotape. San Diego, California: Joel Barker.

Bradley, J., and M. Rotheman. 1989. *Suicide Imminent Danger Assessment and Suicide Risk among Adolescents: A Training Manual for Runaway Shelter Staff.* Unpublished Curriculum.

Brent, D. A. et al. 1988. Risk Factors for Adolescent Suicide. *General Psychiatry* 45: June.

————. 1993. Psychiatric Risk Factors for Adolescent Suicide: A Case Control Study. *Journal of the American Academy of Adolescent Psychiatry.* 27:362-66.

Brown, B. and T. F. Courtless. 1982. *Mentally Retarded Offender.* Rockville, Maryland: National Institute of Mental Health, Center for Studies on Crime and Delinquency.

Brown, L. K. 1991. The Correlates of Planning in Adolescent Suicide Attempts. *Journal of the American Academy of Child and Adolescent Psychiatry.* 30:95-99.

Bureau of Justice Assistance. 1995. *Fact Sheet.*

Bureau of Justice Statistics. 1996. Annual Report. Washington, D.C.

Bush, J. M. 1996. Cognitive Self Change. Unpublished Curriculum. Waterbury, Vermont: Vermont Department of Corrections.

Bush, J. M. and B. Bilodeau. 1993. *Options: A Cognitive Change Program.* Longmont, Colorado: National Intitute of Corrections.

Butts, J. A. and G. J. Halemba. 1996. *Waiting for Justice: Moving Young Offenders Through the Juvenile Court Process.* Pittsburgh, Pennsylvania: National Center for Juvenile Justice.

Callahan. 1993. *Handbook of Diversity Issues.* New York City: Plenum Press.

Calloway, J. 1995. Managing Recreation and Leisure for Juvenile Delinquents. In B. Glick and A. P. Goldstein (Eds.) *Managing Delinquency Programs That Work.* Lanham, Maryland: American Correctional Association.

Cellini, H., B. Schwartz, and S. Readio. 1993. Child Sexual Abuse: An Administrator's Nightmare. In *School Safety Update.* Westlake Village, California: National School Safety Center.

Centers for Disease Control. 1995. Adolescent Suicide: Policy and Strategies. Washington, D.C.: National Institutes of Health.

Clear, T. R. 1995. The Design and Implementation of Classification Systems. *Federal Probation.* 59(2):58-61.

Cumming, Georgia, and Maureen Buell. 1996. *Supervision of the Sex Offender.* Available from American Correctional Association. Lanham, Maryland.

Drapkin, Martin L. 1996. *Developing Policies and Procedures for Jails: A Step-By-Step Guide.* Lanham, Maryland: American Corectional Association.

Drug Abuse Resistance Education (DARE). 1995. Washington, D.C.: Bureau of Justice Assistance.

Ewing, C. P. 1990. *Kids Who Kill.* Lexington, Massachusetts: Lexington Press.

Faiver, Kenneth. 1998. *Health Care Management Issues in Corrections.* Lanham, Maryland: American Correctional Association

Federal Bureau of Investigation. 1974, 1995. Uniform Crime Reports. Washington, D.C.: U.S. Justice Department.

Feindler, E. L. 1979. *Cognitive and Behavioral Approaches to Anger Control Training in Explosive Adolescents.* Unpublished doctoral dissertation. West Virginia University.

————. 1981. The Art of Self Control. Unpublished manuscript. Garden City, New York: Adelphi University.

Feindler, E. L., S. A. Marriott, and M. Iwata. 1984. Group Anger Control Training for Junior High School Delinquents. *Cognitive Therapy and Research.* 8, 299-311.

Finnigan, J. 1995. *Societal Outcomes of Drug and Alcohol Treatment in the State of Oregon – Phase One Report.* Eugene, Oregon: Oregon Department of Substance Abuse Services.

Garfunkel, A. 1989. *Legal Aspects of Health Care Administration.* Rockville, Maryland: Aspen Systems Corp.

Gendreau, P. 1981. Treatment in Corrections: Martinson was Wrong. *Canadian Psychology.* 22:332-338.

Gendreau, P. and D. A. Andrews. 1994. *The Correctional Program Assessment Inventory, 4th Edition.* New Brunswick, Canada: University of New Brunswick.

Gendreau, P. and T. Little. 1994. A Meta-analysis of the Predictors of Offender Recidivism: Assessment Guidelines for Classification and Treatment. Ottawa, Canada: Ministry Secretariat, Solicitor General of Canada.

Gendreau, P. and R. R. Ross. 1981. Correctional Treatment: Some Recommendations for Successful Interventions. *Juvenile and Family Court Journal.* 34:31-40.

Glick, B. 1979. Youth Between the Cracks. *Behavioral Disorders.* 4:227-230.

————. 1983. Juvenile Delinquency. In A. P. Goldstein (Ed.) *The Prevention and Containment of Aggression.* Elmsford, New York: Pergamon Press.

————. 1986. Programming for Juvenile Delinquents: An Administrator's Perspective. In S. J. Apter and A. P. Goldstein (Eds.) *Youth Violence: Programs and Prospects.* Elmsford, New York: Pergamon Press.

Glick, B. and A. P. Goldstein. 1995. *Managing Delinquency Programs that Work.* Lanham, Maryland: American Correctional Association.

Glueck, S. and I. Glueck. 1950. *Unraveling Juvenile Delinquency.* New York, New York: Commonwealth Fund.

Goldstein, A. P. and B. Glick. 1987. *Aggression Replacement Training: A Comprehensive Intervention for Aggressive Youth.* Champaign, Illinois: Research Press.

————. 1989. *Reducing Delinquency: Intervention in the Community.* New York: Pergamon Press.

————. 1994. *The Prosocial Gang: Implementing Aggression Replacement Training.* Thousand Oaks, California: Sage Publications.

Gondles, James A., Jr. 1997. Kids Are Kids, Not Adults. *Corrections Today.* June.

Hayes, L. M., and J. R. Rowan. 1988. *National Study of Jail Suicides: Seven Years Later.* Alexandria, Virginia: National Center on Institutions and Alternatives.

Hendrin, H. 1986. Suicide: A Review of New Directions in Research. *Hospital Community Psychiatry.* 37:148-154.

Hirschi, T. 1969. *Causes of Delinquency.* Newbury Park, California: Sage Publications.

Howard, John. 1973. *The State of Prisons*, 4th Edition. Montclair, New Jersey: Patterson- Smith.

Ingersoll, S. 1997. The National Juvenile Justice Action Plan: A Comprehensive Response to a Critical Challenge. *Juvenile Justice*. 3:2, 11-20.

Jacobs, D. G. 1989. Evaluation and Care of Suicidal Behavior in Emergency Settings. In D. G. Jacobs and H. N. Brown (Eds.) *Suicide: Understanding and Responding*. Harvard Medical School Perspectives on Suicide. Madison, Connecticut: International Universities Press.

Lauen, Roger. 1997. *Positive Approaches to Corrections: Research, Policy, and Practice*. Lanham, Maryland: American Correctional Association.

Leo, Richard A. 1996. *Miranda*'s Revenge: Police Interrogation as a Confidence Game. *Law and Society Review*. 30(2):259-288.

Lipsey, M. W. 1992. Juvenile Delinquency Treatment: A Meta-analysis Inquiry into the Variability Effects. In T. D. Cook, N. Cooper, D. S. Cordray, H. Hartman, L. V. Hedges, R. J. Light, T. A. Louis, and F. Mosteller (Eds). *Meta-Analysis for Explanation*. New York, New York: Russell Sage Foundation. pp. 83-127.

Lyons, J. 1994. *Inmate Suicide Report*. New York: New York State Department of Correctional Services.

Mann, Coramae Richey. 1993. *Unequal Justice: A Question of Color*. Indianapolis, Indiana: University Press.

Marcus, P. et. al. 1993. Characteristics of Suicides by Inmates in an Urban Jail. *Hospital and Community Psychiatry*. 44:3.

Marstellar, F. 1995. *Mental Disorders Among Youth in Georgia Detention Facilities*. Atlanta, Georgia: Emory University Research Project.

Martinson, R. 1974. What Works? Questions and Answers about Prison Reform. *The Public Interest*. 36:22-45.

———. 1978. *A Response to What Works*. Rockville, Maryland: Criminal Justice Clearinghouse.

Marttunen, M. J. et al. 1995. Psychological Stressors More Common in Adolescent Suicides with Alcohol Abuses Compared with Depressive Adolescent Suicides. *Journal of American Academy of Child and Adolescent Psychiatry*. 33:4.

McKay, Rogers, and McKay. 1989. *Journal of Offender Rehabilitation*. 14:3-4:p. 88.

Meichenbaum, D. 1977. *Cognitive Behavior Modification*. New York, New York: Plenum Press.

Meichenbaum, D., B. Gilmore, and A. Fedoravicius. 1971. Group Insight vs. Group Desensitization in Treating Speech Anxiety. *Journal of Consulting and Clinical Psychology*. 36:410-421.

National Association Against Media Violence. 1989. *Television Violence and Assault on Our Children*. Washington, D.C.: National Association Against Media Violence.

National Center on Institutions and Alternatives. 1995. *National Study of Jail Suicides: Seven Years Later*. Alexandria, Virginia: National Center on Institutions and Alternatives.

National Institute of Corrections Planning Session. 1995. Longmont, Colorado: National Institute of Corrections.

National Institute of Justice. 1996. *Research in Brief.*

National Institute of Mental Health. 1982. *Television and Behavior: Ten Years of Scientific Progress and Implications for the Eighties.* Rockville, Maryland: Department of Health and Human Services.

New York State Division for Youth. 1996. *Technical Report.* Rensselaer, New York: Division for Youth.

Novaco, R. W. 1975. *Anger Control: The Development and Evaluation of an Experimental Treatment.* Lexington, Massachusetts: Lexington Press.

————. 1979. Anger and Coping with Stress. In J. Foreyt and D. Rathjen (Eds.) *Cognitive Behavior Therapy: Therapy, Research and Practice.* New York: Plenum Press.

Office of Juvenile Justice and Delinquency Prevention. 1977. Annual Report. p. 99.

————. 1994. Testimony by O'Leary and T. Clear before Congressional Committee for Regulation Revision and Reform.

————. 1995. *Effective Practices in Correctional Education.* Rockville, Maryland: Juvenile Justice Clearinghouse.

————. 1996a. Research Report: *Combating Violence and Delinquency: The National Juvenile Justice Action Plan.* Rockville, Maryland: Juvenile Justice Clearinghouse.

————. 1996b. *State Responses to Serious and Violent Crime.*

Ohio Department of Alcohol and Drug Addiction Services. 1994. Annual Report. Columbus, Ohio.

O'Leary, V. 1977. *Contemporary Sentencing: Policies and Community Corrections.* Albany, New York: University of Albany Press.

O'Leary, V. and T. R. Clear. 1995. *Community Corrections into the 21st Century.* Washington, D.C.: National Institute of Corrections.

Palmer, T. 1978. *Correctional Intervention and Research: Current Issues and Future Prospects.* Lexington, Massachusetts: Lexington Books.

Pederson, P. 1988. *A Handbook for Developing Multicultural Awareness.* Alexandria, Virginia: American Counseling Association.

Rogers, D. 1990. *Adolescent Development.* New York: Houghton Mifflin.

Rosado, Lourdes M. 1996. Minors and the Fourth Amendment: How Juvenile Status Should Invoke Different Standards for Searches and Seizures on the Street. *New York University Law Review.* 71:762-796.

Ross, R., E. Fabiano, and R. Ross. 1986. *Reasoning and Rehabilitation: A Handbook for Teaching Cognitive Skills.* Ottawa, Ontario, Canada: The Cognitive Center.

Roy, A. 1989. *Comprehensive Textbook of Psychiatry/ Vol. 2, Fifth Edition.* Baltimore, Maryland: Williams and Wilkins.

Rutherford, F. and B. Wolford. 1987. *Special Education in the Criminal Justice System.* Columbus, Ohio: Merrill Publishing Company.

Schaffer, D. et al. 1988. *Suicide and Depression in Children and Adolescents.* Boston, Massachusetts: Allyn and Bacon.

School Life. 1962. Washington, D.C.: National Education Association.

Schulz, A. 1995. *Mental Health Status of Juveniles.* Columbus, Ohio: Ohio Department of Youth Services.

Schwartz, B. K. and H. R. Cellini (Eds.) *The Sex Offender: Corrections, Treatment and Legal Practice.* Kingston, New Jersey: Civic Research Institute, Inc.

Seley, H. 1956. *The Stress of Life.* New York: McGraw-Hill Book Company.

Shaffer D. et al. 1974. Suicide in Children and Early Adolescents. *Journal of Psychology and Psychiatry.* 15:275-91.

Shafi, M. et al. 1985. Psychological Autopsy of Completed Suicide in Children and Adolescents. *Journal of Clinical Psychiatry.* 142:1061-64.

Sickmund, M., H. N. Snyder, and E. Poe Yamagata. 1997. *Juvenile Offenders and Victims: 1997 Update on Violence.* Washington, D.C.: Office of Juvenile Justice and Delinquency Prevention.

Soriano, F. I. 1993. Cultural Sensitivity and Gang Intervention. In A. P. Goldstein and C. R. Huff (Eds.) *The Gang Intervention Handbook.* Champaign, Illinois: Research Press.

———. 1995. Cultural Sensitivity in Delinquency Prevention and Intervention Programs. In B. Glick and A. Goldstein (Eds.) *Managing Delinquency Programs that Work.* Lanham, Maryland: American Correctional Association.

Sturgeon, W. and Associates. 1995. Gang Intelligence Web Chart.Pittsfield, Massachusetts: Sturgeon.

Sturgeon, W. et al. 1990. *Prison Security Curriculum.* Longmont, Colorado: National Institute of Corrections.

———. 1993. *Gang Intervention Curriculum for Jails.* Longmont, Colorado: National Institute of Corrections.

Taylor, C. S. 1990. *Dangerous Society.* East Lansing, Michigan: Michigan State University Press.

Taymans, J. and S. Parese.1995. *Problem Solving Skills for Offenders Curriculum.* Longmont, Colorado: National Institute of Corrections.

Travis, L. F. 1982. *Corrections: An Issues Approach.* Cincinnati, Ohio: Anderson Publishing Company.

Travis, L. F. and E. J. Latessa. 1996. Classification and Needs Assessment Module. In *Managing Violent Youthful Offenders in Adult Institutions Curriculum.* Longmont, Colorado: National Institute of Corrections.

U.S. Department of Health and Human Services, National Center for Health Statistics. 1997. (Advanced Report) *Adolescent Sexual Activity.* Vital Statistics. 45(5). Hyattsville, Maryland: Public Health Service.

U.S. Department of Justice. 1984. Attorney General's Task Force on Family Violence: Final Report. Washington, D.C.: U.S. Department of Justice

Utah Department of Corrections. 1994. *Housing Strategies for Serious Youthful Offenders.* Salt Lake City: Utah Department of Corrections.

Widom, C. 1992. *Cycle of Violence*. Washington, D.C.: U.S. Department of Justice.

———. 1995. *Victims of Childhood Sexual Abuse*. Washington, D.C.: National Institute of Justice.

———. 1996. Update Reports. Washington, D.C.: U.S. Department of Justice.

Witt, P. A. and J. Crompton (Eds.) 1996. *Recreation Programs that Work for At-Risk Youth: The Challenge of Shaping the Future*. State College, Pennsylvania: Venture Publishing, Inc.

Wolfgang, M. 1958. An Analysis of Homicide/Suicide. *Journal of Clinical Experimental Psychopathology*. 19:208-218.

Yochelson, S. and S. Samenow. 1976. *The Criminal Personality. Vol. I: A Profile for Change*. New York: Jason Aronson.

Zeigler, W. 1973. *Futures Invention*. Syracuse, New York: Unpublished Workshop.

Appendix 1

Explanation of Terms Used in Survey

Since jurisdictions are independent and create their own statutes relative to juveniles, collecting and collating data is most challenging. To organize this information garnered from the ACA survey, we categorized offenses in broad domains of criminal activity, usually punishable by imprisonment or death.

Capital:
This category refers to capital crimes and includes such offenses as: Murder 1, 2, 3, Manslaughter, Homicide, and, in general, the killing of human beings.

Robbery/Burglary:
These categories refer to property thefts in general, and include: Robbery 1, 2, 3; Burglary, 1, 2, 3; Breaking and Entering; Grand Theft (California); Receiving Stolen Property (California); Forgery/Fraud (California); Stolen Property; Grand Larceny; Shoplifting (Mississippi); Uttering Forgery (Mississippi); Property (Texas); Injuring Jail/Property (Utah).

Sex Crime:
This category includes any and all sexual crimes, such as: Rape 1, 2; Other Sexual Crimes; Lewd Act with Child; Gross, Aggravated/Sexual Imposition (North Dakota); Sexual Contact with Child (South Dakota); Incest (South Dakota); Aggravated Child Abuse; Lewd Lascivious Act in the Presence of a Child (Florida); Forcible Sexual Penetration by Use of a Foreign Object (Idaho); Prostitution; Sexual Exploitation (Washington); Sodomy; Infamous Crimes Against Nature, Committed by Force or Violence (Idaho); Involuntary Deviate Sexual Intercourse (Pennsylvania); and, Indecent Liberties (forcible compulsion) (Washington).

Kidnaping:
This category includes charges such as Abduction (Louisiana); and Missing Persons (California).

Felony:
This is a general category which is inclusive of most of the charges and offenses for which juveniles are being transferred to adult jurisdictions. This category includes offenses such as Felony A, B, C, D, 1, 2, 3; Unclassified Capital (Connecticut); and Criminal Deviate Behavior (Indiana).

Weapons:
This charge refers to the use of dangerous weapons when committing a Felony, Firearms; Armed Felony; Possession of Weapon or Other dangerous Weapon; and Theft of Firearms (Utah).

A&B:
Refers to Assault and Battery and it includes Assault 1, 2, 3; Battery 1, 2, 3; and Assault by Prisoner.

Drugs:
Includes: Controlled Substances Sales and/or Manufacture, Possession; Possession with Intent to Distribute; Marijuana Possession and/or Sales.

Gangs:
Simply refers to statutes which prosecute gang-related behavior. Some statutes include: Soliciting a Minor to Join a Gang (Arkansas); and Criminal Gang Activity and Intimidation (Indiana).

Terrorism:
Includes Terrorist Acts and Mayhem (Idaho).

Pub. Offic.:
This is an interesting category. Although there is an unwritten rule that criminals who victimize public officials will be dealt with more harshly, the codification for this category suggests that there may be an increase in attacks against public officials.

Arson:
Includes offenses such as: Manufacturing Bombs (Connecticut); Arson Involving an Inhabited Structure (North Dakota); Dangerous Use of Explosives (New Mexico); and Incendiary Device (Washington).

Escape:
Refers to those who have escaped from state or other official facilities.

Vehicular:
Refers to crimes committed involving the use of a vehicle such as: Vehicular Manslaughter (California); Vehicular or Automotive Theft (California and Utah); Carjacking (Indiana); Driving While Intoxicated.

Schools:
Refers to crimes committed within or around school premises. Some states actually compel previously adjudicated juveniles to attend school as part of their probation, or else they can be transferred to adult jurisdictions.

Witness:
This category is inclusive of any form of intimidation of witnesses.

Shoplifting:
Although this category has been lumped under robbery and burglary, it is indicative of the expansion of the legal boundaries of transfer protocols.

Riot:
This term has been used in reference to riots initiated inside prisons (Utah).

Treason:
Codified into law in State of Washington.

Extortion:
Includes all forms of extortion.

Other:
This category includes Compounding Crimes (Mississippi); and Construction or Possession of Infernal Machine (Utah); as well as all other nonspecified offenses.

Documented Programming in
Adult Facilities for Juvenile Remands

No Programming:
There is no specific programming for juveniles in adult facilities.

Basic Education:
This consists of basic literacy, high school diploma, as well as General Education Degree (GED), and any other pre-college training.

Vocational Education:
This refers to basic vocational education.

Computers:
California and Connecticut indicated that they used computers to engage young offenders and teach them computer skills while taking advantage of a nontraditional approach to education.

Religious:
This refers to basic religious instruction, and it is inclusive of Judaic, Christian, Muslim, and in some places Native American practices.

Self-help:
Some facilities use self-help strategies as a complementary form of programming.

Job Training:
This refers to teaching job training skills for inmates while they are incarcerated as well as for future employment after they are released.

Boot Camp:
A number of adult correctional systems rely on boot camps, or military training programs.

A/D Abuse:
Alcohol and drug abuse treatment.

Anger:
Anger management and behavior modification.

Individual:
This category refers to individual programming that is designed to meet the individual's particular needs.

Sex Offender:
This category refers to sex-offender programming designed specifically for convicted rapists and other sex offenders.

Cognitive Restructuring:
This refers to programs that attempt to increase offenders' self-esteem and decrease criminal behavior.

Special Education:

This refers to programs mandated for special needs offenders.

Gang:

This program is designed to desensitize gang members from gangs, and gang-related behavior.

HIV Education:

This program seeks to create awareness of Human Immunodeficiency Virus and AIDS-related conditions. It also focuses on safe-sex education.

Relapse:

This program is geared to relapse treatment for either repeat offenders, and/or released offenders.

Parenting:

This program is designed for young parents and issues of parenting in and out of jails and prisons.

Victim Awareness:

This program seeks to create an awareness of the victim and the impact of the offender's crime on his or her victim.

Wellness:

This category refers to program initiatives which focus on the physical, mental, and spiritual well being of the juvenile. It suggests the need for a healthy living experience.

Separate Programs:

This refers to programs held separately from adult programs.

Transition:

This refers to transition-issues training for new juvenile inmates in adult facilities.

Prerelease:

This programming is designed to help the juvenile inmate who is being released to make a transition into society.

Suicide:

This refers to suicide-prevention programs and counseling.

Security Envelope Master Checklist

Name of person(s) conducting inspection:_____

_____

Name of facility inspected:_____

_____

Date _____

I. PERIMETER

FENCE/WALL

1. Material:_____

    _____

2. Condition of material:_____

    _____

3. Condition of poles and anchors:_____

    _____

4. Condition of ground surface beneath fence:_____

    _____

5. Condition of material(s) added to fence wall (such as razor-ribbon):_____

    _____

6. Overall condition of the fence/wall:_____ _____

    _____

7. Area(s) of the fence or wall that need immediate attention:_____

_____

_____

_____

8. Person(s) contacted to repair fence/wall:

Name:_____

Date: _____

9. What security measures are being taken while repairs are needed?

_____

_____

_____

_____

10. List any objects or materials stored against or near the fence/wall:_____

_____

_____

If any, who is going to remove them and when?

Name:_____

Date: _____

Date and time contacted:_____

11. Are there any light poles, trees, or fence poles inside or outside of the perimeter that could be used to escape from or that invade the secure perimeter?

_____

_____

If yes, what should be done to correct the situation? (BE SPECIFIC)_____

_____

If yes, who will be responsible to get the tasks accomplished and when?___

_____

Work date: _____

Name:_____

Date and Time contacted:_____

12. What security measures will be taken until the situation is resolved?_____

_____

_____

_____

GATES

(Any break in the secure perimeter, even a gate, detracts from the overall physical barrier effect and should be scrutinized carefully.)

1. Are there any gates in the fence/wall?_____

2. If yes, the type (pedestrian and/or vehicle) and the number of each type?

   Type:_____ Number:_____

   Type:_____ Number:_____

3. How are the gates operated? Manually or Mechanically? Type:_____

_____

4. What type of locking system is used to secure the gate?_____

_____

5. If the gate is secured by means of a manual locking system, who is responsible

   for the key?_____

_____

6. Is there an emergency key?   Yes:_____   No:_____

If yes, where is the key located? _____

Who checked it?

Name:_____

Date: _____

7. If the locking system is mechanically operated, when was the last time the manual override was checked?

Who checked it?

Name:_____

Date: _____

ELECTRONIC MONITORING OF PERIMETER FENCE/WALL

(Conduct a test on the system to insure it is operating properly. Test will vary depending on the type of system that is being used.)

1. Types:_____

2. Locations:_____

3. Operational at time of inspection?   Yes:_____   No:_____

Date: _____

4. If no, what system was not operational? _____

_____

Why was the system inoperative?_____

_____

_____

How long has the system been out of service?_____

_____

What security measures are being taken while the system is inoperative?

_____

_____

_____

When will the system be operational? _____

_____

5. Is the system still under warranty or is a maintenance contract in effect?

Yes:_____   No:_____

If yes, have the appropriate parties been contacted? Yes:_____ No:_____

If yes, by whom?

Name:_____

Date and time contacted:_____

Date repairs will be completed:_____

PERIMETER LIGHTING

(This portion of the inspection should be conducted at night.)

1. Number of burned out lights:_____

    Location of burned out lights:_____

    _____

    _____

2. Person contacted to replace burned out lights.

    Name:_____

    Date and time contacted:_____

    Number of damaged light fixtures:_____

Location of damaged light fixtures:_____

_____

_____

3. Any observable dark spots or shadowed areas?   Yes:_____ No:_____

If yes, where? (List exact location(s)):_____

_____

_____

 Person contacted to repair or replace damaged light fixtures:

Name:_____

Date and time contacted:_____

4. Will the perimeter lights operate on emergency power?

Yes:_____   No:_____

If no, what security measures can replace them?_____

_____

_____

EXTERIOR DOORS

(Conduct a test of the alarm system(s) on exterior doors.)

1. Number of exterior doors? _____

2. Location of exterior doors? _____

_____

_____

3. Type of material on exterior doors? _____

_____

_____

4. Type(s) of exterior doors:

   Sliders_____

   Swing_____

   Overhead_____

5. Are there door handles on the exterior doors?   Yes:_____   No:_____

6. What types of locking system(s) are employed on the exterior doors?

   Manual:_____

   Mechanical:_____

7. Are exterior doors alarmed?   Yes:_____   No:_____

   If yes, what type of alarms?_____

   _____

   Where does the alarm sound?_____

   _____

   Is the alarm operational at the time of inspection?   Yes:_____   No:_____

   If no, how long has the alarm been out of service?_____

   _____

   Who is responsible for fixing the alarm?_____

   _____

   Date and time contacted:_____

   When is the alarm expected to be back in service? _____

   _____

   How many times in the past calendar year has the alarm system been out

   of service?_____

   _____

8. Describe in detail the problem with the exterior door alarm system. Areas to examine include the following:

Was the system's installation faulty? _____

_____

What days and times has the system malfunctioned? _____

_____

Is the system being sabotaged? _____

_____

If so, by whom? _____

_____

9. What steps are being taken to repair any deficiencies in the exterior doors?

_____

_____

_____

_____

Person contacted: _____

Date and time contacted:_____

10. What security measures are being taken to compensate for deficiencies with exterior doors? _____

_____

_____

_____

_____

11. Does the facility adhere to all the fire and safety codes pertaining to the exterior doors?   Yes:_____   No:_____

If no, where are these violations?_____

_____

_____

Who is responsible for these codes?_____

Date and time contacted:_____

EXTERIOR WINDOWS

1. Number of exterior windows: _____

2. Number of exterior windows that the offenders have direct access to on a
   continuous basis:_____

3. Type of material covering exterior windows to which offenders have access:

   Bars:_____ Chain link:_____

   Expanded metal:_____ Other:_____

   Screening:_____ None:_____

4. List windows where external material is damaged or missing: _____

   _____

5. In your opinion, was the damage to exterior window(s) caused by people?

   Yes:_____ No:_____

   If yes, describe in detail? _____

   _____

   _____

6. To whom has the deficiency been reported?

   Name:_____

   Date:_____

7. What security measures are being taken until the deficiency is repaired?

_____

_____

_____

_____

8. What is the condition of the exterior windows?

_____

_____

_____

_____

Each window should be examined for the following items:

Frames

Note: Some caulking materials are highly flammable and offenders may use pieces of caulking to start fires.

Securely attached to the building?   Yes:_____   No:_____

Caulking material in place but tampered with?   Yes:_____ No:_____

If yes, does the tampering present an immediate security violation?

_____

List any windows missing "O" ring type seals that secure the surface material (the glass) to the frame. List any windows with improper caulking.

_____

_____

_____

Windows

Are there any windows missing or damaged?   Yes:_____ No:_____

Number of missing or damaged windows:_____

Exact location of missing or damaged window(s):_____

_____

_____

_____

_____

_____

_____

Type of window material:

Glass:_____ Polycarbonate:_____

Plastic:_____ Wire:_____

Other:_____

Note: Materials taken from windows often is used to make weapons.

Person to whom exterior window(s) deficiency was reported:

Name:_____ Date:_____

9. In your opinion, is the damage caused by people? Yes:_____ No:_____

If yes, describe in detail:_____

_____

10. What security measures are being taken until the deficiencies are repaired?

_____

_____

_____

_____

_____

_____

II. INTERIOR ALARM SYSTEMS

1. Types:_____

_____

_____

_____

2. What causes the alarm(s) to activate?_____

_____

3. Where does the alarm sound?_____

4. Are all interior alarms operational at the time of inspection? Yes_____ No_____

   If no, how long has the system(s) been out of service?_____

   Why is the system out of service?_____

   _____

5. Is the system under warranty? Yes:_____ No:_____

6. Is the system under a maintenance contract? Yes:_____ No:_____

   If yes to either #5 or #6, name of company:_____

   _____

   Has the responsible company been contaced?   Yes:_____ No:_____

   Name of person contacted:_____

   Date:_____

   If no to either #5 or #6, which alarm systems are not operational?

   _____

   _____

7. If the system is not under warranty or maintenance contract, who is

   responsible for the system's repair? _____

   Date and time contacted:_____

8. What is wrong with the system?_____

_____

_____

9. When will the system be back in service?_____

_____

_____

10. How many times in the past calendar year has the interior alarm system(s)

been out of service?_____

11. Describe in detail the problem(s) with the alarm system(s). _____

_____

_____

Areas to examine include the following:

Is the system's installation faulty? _____

Is the system being sabotaged (if so, by whom)?_____

_____

_____

_____

What days and times has the system(s) malfunctioned? _____

_____

12. What is the staff response time to an alarm?_____

_____

_____

13. Do all alarm systems meet fire and safety codes?   Yes:_____   No:_____

14. List the location of those that do not meet code standards:_____

_____

_____

_____

_____

15. Test each system, then list deficiencies of alarm systems.

    System:_____

    Name:_____ Date:_____

    System:_____

    Name:_____ Date:_____

    System:_____

    Name:_____ Date:_____

16. What security measures are being taken while the system(s) are out
    of service? _____

    _____

    _____

17. What is the anticipated date that the system(s) will be back in service?

    _____

    _____

    _____

III. INTERIOR LIGHTING

One of the most common problems in correctional institutions is burned out lights and damage to lighting fixtures.

1. Number of lights per area:

   (Example: A pod has 12 flourescent ceiling lights, 4 wall mounted corridor lights and 2 flourescent lights in each cell.)

   Number of burned out lights per area (list separately).

   A. POD:_____

   _____

   _____

   B. POD:_____

   _____

   _____

   C. POD:_____

   _____

   _____

   Kitchen:_____

   Main Corridor:_____

   Describe the areas unique to your institution:_____

   _____

   _____

   _____

2. Will interior light operate on emergency power?   Yes_____   No_____

   If no, what security measures are in place to handle this problem?_____

   _____

   _____

   Person contacted to replace burned out lights:

   Name:_____ Date:_____

   Person contacted to repair or replace damaged lighting fixtures:

   Name:_____ Date:_____

IV. CELLS OR INMATE LIVING AREAS

When conducting a cell or inmate living area security check, concern and attention must be given to the physical security of the cell. **This is not a cell search.** If contraband is found, follow institutional policy and procedures for such incidents.

CELL FRONT(S)

1. Locking mechanism(s) is(are) in good working order: Yes:_____ No:_____

   List cell(s) or living area(s) having a problem with their locking system(s):

   _____

   _____

2. How long has the locking system been out of service?_____

   _____

   What appears to be the problem?_____

   Are inmates still being housed in the cell or living area? Yes:_____ No:_____

   If yes, what additional security measures are being taken to compensate for

   the malfunctioning locking system?_____

   _____

   _____

   _____

3. Person contacted to repair or replace locking system:

   Name:_____ Date:_____

4. Anticipated date the system will be back in service:_____

5. Type of cell front or living area doors:

   Bars:_____

   Solid Door (metal or wood):_____

   Solid Door with observation window:_____

6. Overall condition of cell front or living area door:

Bars solid and intact: Yes:_____   No:_____

Check bars to insure they have not been cut: Yes:_____   No:_____

Hinges intact and operate easily: Yes:_____   No:_____

Sliders on track and easily open: Yes:_____   No:_____

Doors (exterior and interior) intact: Yes:_____   No:_____

Observation windows intact: Yes:_____   No:_____

INTERIOR WALLS, CEILINGS, AND FLOORS

1. Construction:

Cinder block:_____

Concrete:_____

Stone:_____

Brick:_____

Painted. Yes:_____   No:_____

Overall condition of cell walls, ceiling, and floors:_____

_____

_____

2. Service materials intact? Yes:_____   No:_____

If no, list deficiencies and exact location(s):_____

_____

_____

(Check for scratches on walls and floors. Multiple scratches could indicate that inmates are sharpening objects into weapons.)

COMMODES

1. Are commodes securely fastened to the wall and floor?

Yes:_____ No:_____

If no, identify the problem area:_____

_____

_____

Molding and/or caulking around commode intact and made up of the

same material: Yes:_____ No:_____

Commode and sink in good working order (conduct test):

Yes:_____ No:_____

(Be careful to examine closely push type flushing mechanism on commodes and push type faucets on sinks to insure that the button and the rod is attached and cannot be pulled back through the cell.)

BEDS

1. Beds are securely anchored to the wall and/or floor?   Yes:_____ No:_____

2. Are all anchor bolts in place?   Yes:_____ No:_____

3. Bed assemblies are complete with no parts missing?   Yes:_____ No:_____

CELL LIGHTING

1. Is lighting functioning at time of inspection?   Yes:_____ No:_____

2. Are lighting fixtures intact: Yes:_____ No:_____

ELECTRICAL OUTLETS

1. Are electrical outlets functioning at time of inspection? Yes:_____ No:_____

2. Are outlet covers appropriately installed?   Yes:_____ No:_____

3. Person contacted to repair and/or replace deficiencies in outlets:

Name:_____

Date:_____

HALLWAYS

1. Number of doors leading off hallway: _____

2. Are doors secure at time of inspection?   Yes:_____ No:_____

3. Number of utility access doors in hallway:_____

    Were utility access doors secured at time of inspection?

    Yes:_____ No:_____ Not Applicable:_____

4. Number of windows in hallway:_____

    Condition of windows and frames in hallway: (*Be specific as to any damaged*

    or missing windows.)_____

    _____

    _____

    _____

    _____

    _____

5. Cleanliness of hallway(s) at time of inspection. (List any deficiencies.)

    _____

    _____

    _____

V. KITCHEN/DINING AREA

1. Construction:

   Cinder block:_____

   Concrete:_____

   Stone:_____

   Painted:_____

   Paneled:_____

   Other:_____

2. Number of doors leading to kitchen/dining area:_____

   Type of doors: _____

   _____

3. Type of locking systems on doors (be specific):_____

   _____

4. Were doors secure at time of inspection?   Yes:_____ No:_____

5. Method of securing cutting utensils:_____

   _____

   _____

   _____

6. Were any cutting utensils left lying around during time of inspection?

   Yes:_____ No:_____

7. The inventory of cutting utensils was correct at time of inspection:

   Yes:_____ No:_____

   If no, what security measures are to be taken (be specific):_____

   _____

8. Number of windows in kitchen/dining area:_____

9. Identify any windows and frames in kitchen/dining area needing repair

   or replacement:_____

   _____

   Person contacted to repair deficiencies in the kitchen/dining area:

   Name:_____ Date:_____

VI. HALLWAYS

1. Construction:

   Cinder block:_____

   Concrete:_____

   Stone:_____

   Brick:_____

   Painted:_____

   Unpainted:_____

   Paneled:_____

   Other:_____

2. Overall condition of hallway(s) (give locations):

   _____

   _____

3. List any deficiencies in the condition of the walls, floors, and ceilings:_____

   _____

   _____

   _____

VII. CONTROL ROOM

1. Construction:

   Cinder block:_____

   Concrete:_____

   Stone:_____

   Brick:_____

   Other:_____

2. Describe any deficiencies in the control room ceiling, walls, windows, floors

   (be specific):_____

   _____

   _____

3. Number of T.V. monitors in the control room:_____

4. Were all the monitors functionsing at the time of the inspection?

   Yes:_____   No:_____

   If no, describe why monitor(s) was/were not in operation:_____

   _____

   _____

5. How long have the monitors been out of service?_____

6. Are the monitors under contract?   Yes:_____   No:_____

7. Are the monitors under a maintenance agreement?   Yes:_____ No:_____

   Person contacted to repair the monitors:

   Name:_____   Date:_____

8. What security measures are in place while the monitors are out of service?

_____

_____

9. Conduct a test of **ALL** alarm monitoring systems housed in the control room and list results:

System A: (identify):_____

_____

System B: (identify):_____

_____

Identify any system that is not functioning properly:_____

_____

_____

Are the malfunctioning system(s), if any:

Under contract?   Yes:_____   No:_____

Under a maintenance agreement?   Yes:_____   No:_____

Under a leased agreement?   Yes:_____   No:_____

Person contacted to repair system:

Name:_____   Date:_____

What security measures are being taken until the malfunctioning system is back in service?_____

_____

10. In the event of a power failure in the control room, is the control room on emergency power?   Yes:_____   No:_____

VIII. VISITING AREA

1. Construction:

   Cinder block:_____

   Concrete:_____

   Stone:_____

   Brick:_____

   Other:_____

2. Number of windows:_____

3. Type of visiting:_____

   Contact:_____

   Noncontact:_____

4. Method of separating inmates from visitors in noncontact visit situation:

   _____

   _____

   _____

   _____

   _____

   _____

5. Is the visiting policy conspicuously posted for visitors to see?

   Yes:_____   No:_____

IX. SUMMARY

During the inspection, the following deficiencies were found that **require immediate attention:** (LIST EACH AREA AND BE SPECIFIC)

A follow-up inspection should be conducted and a report written Indicating progress toward correcting deficiencies provided

By _____ Date_____

The following individuals have been interviewed, provided information about the deficiencies Indicated herein, and are designated responsible to manage the corrective action:

Name: _____ Date_____

Deficiency:_____

Name: _____ Date_____

Deficiency:_____

Name: _____ Date_____

Deficiency:_____

Name: _____ Date_____

Deficiency:_____

Name: _____ Date_____

Deficiency:_____

Name: _____ Date_____

Deficiency:_____

Name: _____ Date_____

Deficiency:_____

Name: _____ Date_____

Deficiency:_____

Index

About the Authors

Barry Glick, Ph.D., NCC is a national consultant to criminal justice agencies and formerly the Associate Deputy Director for Local Services with the New York State Division for Youth. Dr. Glick has devoted his career to the study and exploration of adolescents, especially those who are aggressive and violent. Dr. Glick has three decades of experience designing, developing, administering, and managing programs for juvenile delinquents and youthful offenders. He has authored numerous articles and books including *Aggression Replacement Training: A Comprehensive Intervention for Aggressive Youth; The Pro-Social Gang: Implementing Aggression Replacement Training;* and *Managing Delinquency Programs that Work.* Dr. Glick has served in both the public and private sectors of the juvenile justice system and has held positions as a child care worker, psychologist, facility director, regional manager, and agency executive administrator. He received his Doctorate in Counseling Psychology from Syracuse University and is a board certified national counselor. He holds membership in several professional organizations, including the American Correctional Association.

William Sturgeon has over twenty-five years of experience in the criminal justice field. During his career, he has held management positions in both law enforcement and corrections. He has been a consultant for the National Institute of Corrections in the areas of training, management, supervision, and security. Mr. Sturgeon received his bachelor's degree from Southern Vermont College, a master's degree from Goddard College, and training in conflict management and mediation from the Harvard School of Public Health. He is currently Special Assistant to the Director of the South Carolina Department of Corrections.

Charles R. Venator-Santiago is a doctoral candidate in political science at the University of Massachusetts (Amherst). His areas of specialization are public law, political theory, and comprehensive politics. He has a master's degree in political science and has applied his knowledge to international issues involving cultural identity and the law. He was born and raised in Puerto Rico.